Animal Wisdom

*Conversations of the Heart between
Animals and Their People*

Wendy Van de Poll, MS, CEOL

Spirit Paw Press, LLC
Concord, New Hampshire, USA

Animal Wisdom
Conversations of the Heart between Animals and Their People

Published by Spirit Paw Press, Concord NH 03303

Cover design: GermanCreative
Layout & Prepress: Lighthouse24

Publisher's Cataloging in Publication Data
provided by Five Rainbows Cataloging Services

Names: Van de Poll, Wendy, author.
Title: Animal wisdom : conversations of the heart between animals and their people / Wendy Van de Poll.
Description: Concord, NH : Spirit Paw Press, 2018.
Identifiers: ISBN 978-0-9990163-8-1 (softcover)
Subjects: LCSH: Human-animal communication. | Human-animal relationships. | Channeling (Spiritualism) | Spiritualism. | Wisdom. | BISAC: PETS / Essays & Narratives. | BODY, MIND & SPIRIT / Channeling & Mediumship. | BODY, MIND & SPIRIT / Spiritualism.
Classification: LCC QL85 .V36 2018 (print) | LCC QL85 (ebook) | DDC 591.5--dc23.

Disclaimer

This work is based on actual Animal Wisdom sessions. The participants featured in this book have granted legal permission for inclusion of their stories. Some names and identifying details have been changed to protect the privacy of individuals.

THANK YOU!

Thank you for purchasing *Animal Wisdom: Conversations of the Heart between Animals and Their People.*

To show my appreciation, I'm offering an audio chapter—Don't Mess with My Happiness—from the international bestselling book *Choosing Happiness* where I share the story of how my dog Marley reminded me to come home to myself.

Visit https://wendyvandepoll.com/
to download your FREE GIFT

This book is dedicated to those animals who are my co-authors. Thank you for sharing your deepest thoughts and wisdom. And to their people for loving, caring, and listening.

Axle   Baby   Bell   Bonnie

Charlie Girl   Chris   Coco   Francis

Gerri   Hampton   July Mae   Lilly

Max   Marley   Miss Electra   Miss Luna

Miss Pepper   Myrtle   Oliver   Oscar

Peetie   Randy   Rascal   Riley

Ruby   Sally   Storm

Thomas   Zorah

Contents

Introduction

Are you an animal lover who shares the belief your animal is in your life for a special reason? Do you wonder what this reason may be?

In this book I will share 30 Animal Wisdom Messages from pets to their people. Each one is unique, compassionate, and honest. If you are a person who wants support, guidance, and inspiration on how your animal can help you heal your blocks and discover your life purpose, this book's 30 Animal Wisdom Messages will inspire you to consider the human-animal bond in a different and more profound way.

In this down-to-earth book you will experience respect, seriousness, fairness, humor, compassion, and even moments of silliness regarding the insights beloved pets deliver to their people. You will get to join in the healing journeys of people and their animal companions as they share words of wisdom to build trust and deepen their relationships.

When you read these Animal Wisdom Messages, you, the reader, will gain compassion and support with your own journey, and you will begin to listen to your beloved companion in a new way.

Message Origins

If you are wondering, "How were these animals able to communicate with their people? Where did these messages come from?" then let me explain.

I used my ability as an animal communicator or interspecies conversationalist (see glossary for definition) to talk with these beloved animals and their people via energy. Animal communication is telepathic communication that involves the transmission of thoughts from an animal to the communicator so that they can sense the animal's feelings, intentions, thoughts, mental images, emotions, impressions, sensations, and intuition. As an animal communicator I have the ability to have a soul-level conversation with animals, either living or those that have died, via this proficiency.

As a professional animal communicator and medium I have listened to what animals have been telling me for over 50 years. I started young, yet it wasn't until my adult years that I finally trusted how their wisdom could actually provide sound advice on how to live my life in a more cohesive and productive way.

In fact, my dog Marley taught me the necessary details on how to pay attention to the choices I made for continued happiness. Her compassion never let me down.

As a professional animal communicator for over 20 years, a certified end-of-life and pet loss grief coach (CEOL), licensed massage therapist for humans, horses, and hounds, and wolf biologist, I have consulted with and taught numerous people from around the world to listen and respect what their animals know about them.

I should add too that to hear Animal Wisdom Messages you don't need special powers. Animal communication and these messages are actually available to everyone. If you start with an open heart and soul, and trust your intuition, you too will hear what your animal knows.

When I first offered the service of Animal Wisdom Messages to my community, I had no plan for these messages to eventually be incorporated into a book. At the time, I had over a hundred participants. Halfway through however, the animals began to ask if their words of wisdom could be shared with the world at large. When animals talk—I listen. That is the reason for this book.

A Door to the Sacred

When you read this book, you are engaging with the sacred bond between over two dozen animals and their people, which has changed many human-animal relationships. These animals have helped their people change their frames of mind in regards to trusting their choices and decisions.

As JS, who received two Animal Wisdom Messages, from her dog, Coco, explained it:

> Wendy,
>
> Thank you for the beautiful and amazing session that you shared with Coco. It was such a gift and I appreciate your time, insight, and experience. I cried tears of joy and gratitude. I feel so blessed.
>
> I have reread your record of the session a few times and have had several aha moments. Coco is such a wise soul, and I love her so much. I have told her many times she has saved my life. She is my teacher, and I feel it is time to really open to my intuitive gifts.

I just love what she shared, and I am excited about connecting with her, using her guidance. I know we share a deep love and bond. She has helped me through some very difficult years. It has not been easy. I laughed about the baby talk! I needed to hear that.

I have been told I have healing hands. It was so nice to hear that. I do feel Coco is very receptive when I massage her. She is truly reminding me to find the truth of who I am. When I bless her she always responds, as if saying, "Namaste," to me. She is amazing!

I am so happy I reached out to you. I know there is more I could write, but please know I am so grateful.

I may sign up for another session!

Thank you,

JS

Our animals offer us endless possibilities to become better at being human. By listening to all the animals around you, especially your pet, your life may evolve for both you and them.

For this reason, I'm including a very special chapter in this book with messages from my own beloved dog Marley. Marley was a beautiful Samoyed whom I call the Divine Ms. M. She died a tragic yet powerful and life-changing death. I learned from Marley that happiness was and is there for me always— by trusting my own wisdom through her teachings.

This book that you are about to read will help you feel aware, confident, healthy, and loving for yourself because so many elements of these messages are universal.

Remember, your beloved companion really does want to talk with you. By experiencing the Animal Wisdom Messages in this book, I hope you will be inspired to find out what your animal has to share with you.

Respectfully,

Wendy Van de Poll

January 17, 2018

1—Integrity and Introspection

Since our souls are combined, I give you my confidence and groundedness, that strong sense of self that is centered and respected by all.

—Belle, the dog

Intuitive Conversation with Wendy

As I connect in with Belle she brings me straight into her eyes and deep into her soul. It's of utmost importance for her to show me how complete she is. How grounded she is. How content she is.

There is something special about Belle's energy, which will be discovered when she shares her wisdom with PM.

She is showing me that her soul is huge—her heart is HUGE. In her presence she commands respect for herself as well as anyone sharing her space. Her command is not forceful, but it's a solid presence awash with introspection.

She is incredibly gentle, and her wisdom goes beyond eternity.

It's not by mistake that Belle and PM were in each other's lives. There are many lessons they have learned and will continue to learn.

She is telling me that she is ready to talk with PM.

Intuitive Wisdom Message from Belle to PM

Mom, as I look at you, from where I stand in the universe, I want you to know that I'm not any different really from what my personality was like in the physical with you.

There are many things to share with you, but first I want to let you know I'm okay and I'm present in your world every single day.

I watch and see you clearly from where I am now. I oftentimes crawl into your heart and into your soul to comfort you. I'm close whenever you need me. My big soul is part of you. Please remember that we are forever soul-buddies.

My intelligence is respected here in the afterlife, as is my fairness. Do you remember how fair I was in the physical realm? I would like you to remember once again how I presented myself to you and others. When you remember this, your groundedness will be stronger.

As you know I was also honest and strong. This, along with my groundedness and fairness, is my truth. I want to thank you because you gave me this gift. Did you know that? I didn't have this before you. But it was my life destiny to be with you. I needed you—I needed you to help me feel secure and confident.

I hope you realize you're helping me be that great dog with all these wonderful attributes. My gift to you is the same.

Since our souls are combined, I give to you the same confidence, groundedness, and strong sense of self that is respected by all. Integrity, introspection, fairness, and confidence—these are your words to live by.

You told Wendy you miss me, and that's understandable. I miss you too. But I'm not far away. I'm still in your heart, and remember, I'm your soul, so we share the same thoughts.

I want you to know that you can talk to me. You can ask me questions. You can write me letters of love and appreciation.

It is important for me to share with you because I think you forget sometimes. You are perfect just the way you are, and I loved sharing my life with you. I still do—even though it's different.

In the stillness of our love and the stillness of our hearts please remember the stillness of your mind. Reach out to me whenever you need support, guidance, and love.

Together we were in the physical. Together we *are* in energy. Together we *are* in love. Together we *are* with grounded forces.

I want you to know here in the afterlife I am being celebrated because I was successful in my Soul Promise (see glossary for definition) to myself and to you. I accomplished what I needed to know. I accomplished what I needed to learn to help you learn the same. I am rewarded greatly for the job that I did.

Thank you, Mom, and I am forever grateful that we got to share life with each other in the physical. I look forward to our relationship as it continues. Let's always communicate with our hearts and souls.

In fairness and confidence,

Belle

Love Note to Belle from PM

Dear Belle,

Thank you for talking with me and for being such a big presence in my life. Your comforting words let me know that you are happy helping other dogs, and you still have a connection with me. Your words from the afterlife have eased my heart.

Your death was a heavy loss for me. Not knowing what you were doing was causing me anxiety. But your words and wisdom give me comfort. Your spirit is in my heart and will never die. We'll always be connected.

Until we meet again,

PM

Critical Insight

While Belle communicated several relevant observations to PM, here's a critical insight from her that everyone can benefit from:

Integrity, introspection, fairness, and confidence—these are your words to live by.

2—Awareness of NOW

When you start feeling like you don't have quality in your life, that means you're going too fast. It's important for you to manage this.

—Storm, the cat

Storm was a domestic, shorthair, male cat. He was a rescue. He died at 11.5 years old. I connected with him in the spirit realm.

Intuitive Conversation with Wendy

Storm connected with my Spirit Team (see glossary for definition) immediately. There was a rush of information, but the most important part was—Storm is a sage—a Zen master. He was dutiful with carrying out his spiritual role on this planet. As he continues his dedication to this role in the afterlife, he reminds his person, CD, he is not far away.

Storm also shows me he's serious and calculating before he decides to move ahead with any decision. He asks this of CD as well.

He holds an extremely high-level spiritual role in the afterlife, which demands reverence and respect. He's part of a council that makes decisions for all types of animals, specifically, in regard to where these animals should journey next.

Intuitive Wisdom Message from Storm to CD

I would like to tell you, mom, it's important for you to be clear—to be clear in your worklife and life work. Do not just trust your decisions on a whim. Try not to go back and forth because that creates chaos in your mind. Be real. Be patient. Be strong!

Your heart is huge but tender. Your big heart gets you into energetic trouble sometimes because you allow too much in. Your filter needs to be strengthened. Without this strengthening your filter will not buffer you. You could become weak and overwhelmed. You will feel like it's your fault when it is not.

Something that you can learn from me when we spent our physical time together is being in the NOW. Being present is critical—not going into the past and not going into the future. Because that is not going to help you stay focused on the NOW and what you're doing in the moment. This will give you the quality of life you so desire.

When you start feeling like you don't have quality in your life, that means you're going too fast. That means your mind is going too fast. That means you're possibly even affected by some of the stuff you absorb from others.

It is important for you to manage this. Understand this is the gift that I can give you because I was so good at that in the physical and still am in the afterlife. I am able to monitor what I want/ed in my realm. I want this for you too.

I was/am clear about my actions, and I'm accountable. I sometimes wasn't the kindest or the most tactful, but I was true to myself—and that's what's important to you. It may be a little rocky as you develop this a little bit further, but it will calm you in the long run. And I'm here to help you keep this in mind.

As you continue to do this you will gain your strength, purpose, and approach to life. It's in the lessons I taught you. You will get there.

The fear that you have is a sign for you. It's a good sign for you as are the other emotions that come up within the sphere of self-doubt. Trust your anger and all of those feelings—keep in mind those are good signs that will remind you to come home to your center.

All that matters is where you are NOW, not where you were in the past or where you're going in the future. Keep the present moment in your space, and your mind chaos will settle. I promise you: your life will become even more beautiful than it is.

You are a wonderful soul and your wisdom is to help the world be a better place. You have been doing this well, but there is a shift that needs to happen in order for you to continue helping others.

If the shift is not taken, you won't be working in the NOW and you will become overwhelmed. Learn who your Spirit Team is and listen to their voices and mine. The universe will buffer and allow for change to happen in your world.

Please understand your intuition and learn how to stay in the NOW. This is key to recognizing your emotional signs of frustration, pain, and loneliness. See these as well as chaos as signs and teachers to embrace a relationship with yourself.

You gave me a relationship, which rescued me. You allowed me to develop and have a home. I am NOW, and who I was in the physical is allowing me to continue to teach you and remind you of the beautiful YOU.

Breathing in the NOW,

Storm

Love Note to Storm from CD

Dear Storm,

Your words of wisdom are helping me so much. Your advice about the relationship between the quality of my life and my mind's tendency to "go too fast" has given me awareness and the ability to slow my mind down. This advice helps me be present to what is happening around me. Your commitment to helping me with this is very comforting to me.

Storm you are my Soul Pet (see glossary for definition). It brings tears to hear all that I did for you. I lovingly gave you a safe home and gave you the space to develop with confidence.

You continue to be with me to teach and remind me to stay in the NOW!

With presence,

CD

Critical Insight

While Storm communicated several relevant observations to CD, let's pay special attention to this one:

Slow down to recognize your wisdom.

3—Whispers from Two Hearts

I love my little whispers in my ear from you. I
want you to imagine and feel those whispers too.
—Bonnie, the dog

Bonnie was a Shih Tzu rescue dog. She was 13 when she died. She was in the spirit world when I connected with her.

Intuitive Conversation with Wendy

As I connect with Bonnie she shows me her gentle soul. She is a pure bundle of love that expands beyond her little body's confines.

Extremely excited she quickly tells me she's sweet, loving, and kind. Bonnie also tells me she's always had a kind word to share with any person that came her way. She loved everything. Bonnie is all about love, love, love!

She loved to be warm, cuddled, and embraced. She loved the little whispers in her ear that CT, her person, gave her. They made her feel good, comfortable, and safe.

It is important for Bonnie to let us know how smart she is and that she could/can figure out anything. Her cunningness was important to her and to CT. There is wisdom in her cunningness.

Intuitive Wisdom Message from Bonnie to CT

I want to thank you for talking with me today, Mom. I have wanted to reach out to you, and I have. Now you will finally hear what I have to tell you.

I loved those little whispers in my ear from you. I want you to imagine those whispers now. I want you to hear as you feel those whispers on your lips again. I know you can as I am still in your heart. Just talk with me. As you whisper to me I want you to write down all those little things that you used to tell me. This will heal your heart.

Writing things down that you whisper to me will remind you how to reconnect with me. Always keep in mind and in your heart that our love is shared between us and is forever. Your love notes will keep us together.

I know you are feeling a little empty right now, but when you write down all those little things that you told me—whispered to me—kissed me with—I am going to return and place them into your heart.

You're going to remember them, and that's going to fill your heart again—because I am never gone. This is all you need to know to contact me.

You came into my life at an important time—you rescued me! I was not happy; I was not well taken care of. But you came at the right time. I was asking for somebody like you to come and find me because I knew I had a bigger purpose in life. I knew I wasn't living my purpose before you came to get me. And I was sad.

But when I saw you, my heart and soul soared to happiness. I knew that my Soul Person (see glossary for definition) had arrived. I want to thank you for letting me be me—at any cost. You allowed me to develop into the sweet, kind, loving, and cunningly smart little being I am.

But honestly, I'm not that little—even though I'm a little dog. Here in the afterlife my energy is big. I'm bossing everybody around in the afterlife—don't worry, it's in a nice way—because I am fair, smart, and loving.

My job here in the afterlife is to help people and other animals know where they should go as soon as they cross over. I help them go to the right place—that's a big job!

And I got this job because you gave me guidance, you gave me permission, and you gave me the space to be who I am supposed to be.

Keep this in mind: I came into your life when you needed a heart dog—when you needed someone to say kind things to you and help you become clearer on your life direction and choices.

In my final message to you for today: know that I am never ever going far away from you. Once again feel the gentle whispers from your lips when you told me about love, trust, and safety.

Don't forget to write those words down. Keep them close to your heart and bring them out when you need to read them again: whenever you feel lonely, sad, or happy! This is my gift to you to always remember why I came into your life. To heal you too! Just like you did for me!

This energy continues—it never goes away—the gentle whispers on our lips as we share our love, kindness, wisdom, and the beautiful ability to be kindly cunning.

Remember, I'm always my sassy little self; embrace that in yourself too!

Softly yours,

Bonnie

Love Note to Bonnie from CT

Dear Bonnie,

You came to me after my first dog died. You were criminally neglected and were, at first, timid. But now you are more confident.

Having you in my life helped me so much. It is a comfort to know that you are happy in the afterlife. You were such a joy here on earth, and I'm pleased to know you are helping others in the afterlife.

And yes, I will still talk to you like I did when we cuddled on the lounge, and I remember your love.

Gently yours,

CT

Critical Insight

While Bonnie communicated many insights, draw your attention to this one:

Love is your kindness.

4—Taming the Mind Chatter

Our first step to helping each other is to balance our energy. We can do this for each other, as we are healers together.

—Gerri, the cat

Gerri is a grey, shorthair, female cat. She is alive and 15 years old.

Intuitive Conversation with Wendy

As Gerri and I begin our conversation I am in awe of her beautiful soul. I see an incredible amount of life and living knowledge for CA, her person. She has wisdom not only in her heart but in her solar plexus (located in the abdominal area) as well.

It's important for her to show me her energy system—precisely her chakra (see glossary for definition) system. Her crown chakra (located in the crown of the head) is enlightened by bright, full light. It exudes deep and profound healing abilities.

She asks me to look at all her chakras. I proceed to do so because it's important for her.

As I see her energy centers or chakras she shows me CA's energy and chakra system as well. They are much alike. She is telling me she would like to be put into balance. She asks if I can do this. I tell her I can, but it will also need to be done by CA on a regular basis. When CA does this for her, she will be helping herself as well. She is CA's healer and mind-chatter tamer.

Gerri is showing me how much she and CA are connected. There are lessons to learn to help each other. This one is the first.

Intuitive Wisdom Message from Gerri to CA

I would like to thank you, Mom, for being willing to talk with me and hear what I want to share. Our first step to helping each other is to balance our energy. We can do this for each other, as we are healers together.

Yes, there are many other things we could talk about, but for today it's about spending time with each other and the balance we have with the physical environment.

Let's talk about our chakras. I showed Wendy my crown chakra how bright mine is. I also showed her yours. They are not the same but close in terms of brightness. We need to make sure our crown chakras are in balance because our brightness determines our happiness.

Both of our heart chakras are strong. Yours comes first in strength. My heart comes in second for strength. I know you move from your heart, and your heart is beautiful. Sometimes the move from your heart is almost too strong. What happens next is your other energy centers don't follow. That's why you get tired, off-centered, and overwhelmed.

The other chakra that needs to be brought into balance is our solar plexus. Ours are spinning too quickly and can cause our tummies to feel upset sometimes.

We need to have our chakras be in balance because when our chakras are unbalanced, it can make certain situations in our lives out of balance too. It can confuse us. It can make it difficult for us to feel at ease. The mind-chatter can take over. If we don't have our energy centers balanced, our lives become drastically off-key, and we can become confused or upset easily. Physical disorders can happen.

I would like you to help me to balance my chakras and to balance your own. Your life will change as will mine as long as we start here. We can start somewhere else, but the final outcome or the process outcome will not be the same.

You see, Mom, your intuition and centered soul come from balancing your chakras.

Balancing our energy centers together is important to do. It's the whispering of our souls. It's the whispering of how we move together on this planet. You see, Mom, it's really important we do this, not only for ourselves, individually, but for each other too. It will help you feel more at peace with your mind and heart. And it will help me as an elder.

I want to give you this gift of balance, so you can experience a more settled life, so you can give more light to life, and simply as a way to show my thankfulness to you.

I am here to help, guide, and give you a way to move forward. We can both move forward with more peace and effectiveness in our daily lives. Being in balance within our physical world is our job together.

The gratitude that we have for life is huge, and we can do many great things together and apart. It takes managing energy. But even if you try with meditation or anything else—

at this point it will be really difficult. We need to start with balancing our energy chakras together.

Love from all of life,

Gerri

Love Note to Gerri from CA

Dear Gerri,

You are a marvel of intuitiveness. I love how you always know exactly what you need and seek me out, insisting that I pay attention to what you have to offer.

You are the sentinel—the one who is first to converse with me every morning. With my feet on the floor you are right there—kneading my legs and looking straight into my eyes. I appreciate your insistence that it is "time for action, Mom!"

You are a true wonder, and I feel so marvelous when you are near. I believe in your powerful healing possibilities.

Love,

CA

Critical Insight

Give special attention to this particular insight from Gerri:

Move forward with peace in your heart to feel joy.

5—Five Lessons for Joy

When your joy, groundedness, and intuition flow,
then your heart is joined with your all-knowing.
This is your key to living life to its fullest.

—Miss Pepper, the cat

As a kitten, Miss Pepper was found by a nursing home resident. When that resident died, Miss Pepper ran to the window, which shows her keen awareness of the passing of that human soul. After this, CD adopted her.

Miss Pepper, a female feline, was 7.5 years old when she died. It was sudden and without warning. Miss Pepper was in the spirit realm when we connected.

Intuitive Conversation with Wendy

What strikes me about Miss Pepper is—she's all pink; she's all girl. She is showing me glittery, white, shiny light with silver and pastels. Her energy and light is all about femininity, strength, and loveliness.

She's delightful, calm, respectful, and tremendously intuitive. She comes to me and cuddles in my lap—she likes that feeling.

The thing about Miss Pepper, she is more etheric than physical. Always has been. The physical for her was just temporary. She had two quick tasks—the person in the nursing home and YOU.

Intuitive Wisdom Message from Miss Pepper to CD

Not to worry that I had a short life. I lived in the physical just as long as I needed. My job was to gather information. It was important for me to learn from you and my other person what actually happens on the physical plane.

You see, I am a light being. I am about inspiration, etheric groundedness, and creativity. I believe in moving from the heart and watching over the world. I enjoy this tremendously, and you gave me the safety and space to fine-tune my abilities.

I'm not your normal kitty, you do know that, right?

You shared with Wendy that I'd been living in a nursing home with a resident and that I'd followed her soul out. Yes, you were right. She was one of my teachers—as are you.

I learned much from you. You helped me put together the lessons I learned from my other person. I have new lessons from you too, and I will tell you about them shortly.

I died when I did because it was time for me to leave my physical body. You actually did give me what I needed. My death is okay, so please don't worry about me.

Here are your new lessons from me:

1. I ask you to listen to your intuition and make sure you are aware of how you diffuse and buffer the energy around you. Since you already taught me how to do this, it shouldn't be difficult for you to do.

2. Learn how to incorporate your intuition, so you are more available for yourself. You understand this, but there's some fine-tuning to do that I can help you with. Awareness is important.

3. The third consideration is flow—use your intuition to slowly integrate all that you receive. Integrate the ebb and flow of your energy. You allowed me to flow with my practice while I was healing your heart. Consider the ocean—listen to the ocean to feel what I mean.

4. Keep close the warmth in our hearts that we have for each other and ourselves! When I was "lost," you took me home, and your warmth spilled into my heart. I lost a person and a teacher. I tried to follow their soul. But I couldn't! You saw that and rescued me. It is because of that my heart was healed, and I am forever thankful. My gift to you is for your heart to feel warm inside just like you made mine. Trust your heart...I do.

5. Integrate the lessons of all-knowingness. As you know—I am all-knowing. I only had to live in the physical for 7.5 years. That's all I needed. I needed to live with that other person because I needed to feel like I could take care of somebody. With my all-knowing personality I know that you do that too, and you can do that even more as you integrate the lessons from today.

As you ponder my wisdom and teachings please observe our/your strength. Watch yourself as you use your intuition and look for the energy flow to bring you forward. As you bring in the energy of your heart, use your abilities of all-knowingness.

This, my friend, is a great gift that you have. When your joy, groundedness, and intuition flow, then your heart is joined with your all-knowingness. This is your key to living life to its fullest.

Thank you for letting me be in your life for a short period of time and for taking care me.

Respectfully,

Miss Pepper

Love Note to Miss Pepper from CD

Dear Miss Pepper,

Your encouragement is invaluable. Your words of wisdom about my joy, etheric groundedness, intuition, flow, heart, and all-knowingness as the key to my living to the fullest has encouraged me.

Your help and support have convinced me to listen to my inner voice that guides me.

Encouraged,

CD

Critical Insight

Let's notice in particular that Miss Pepper communicated this wise message:

Choose only those situations that create fullness in your life.

6—Joyful Trust for the Heart

You gave me the space. You gave me safety. You gave me heart to trust in myself. I'm asking you to share your heart with peace and joy, but never ever forget who you are inside.

—Charlie Girl, the dog

Charlie Girl was a female Miniature Schnauzer mix. She was 15 when she died. She was a rescue. She was in the spirit realm when we connected for this conversation.

Intuitive Conversation with Wendy

I'm getting a lot of fun energy from Charlie Girl. She is playful, high-spirited, and happy. She also has another side that's quiet and smart. But she's telling me she prefers the fun part of herself.

In the afterlife she has reached an understanding. She feels safe and protected. She tells me she really didn't want to leave MAS, her person, just yet.

She's thankful for the wisdom that MAS helped her develop. Charlie Girl didn't have much before her person came into her life and opened the door for her. MAS gave her a tremendous amount of support and love. She is saying she appreciates MAS and that MAS is quite beautiful.

Right now, Charlie Girl is jumping up and down, going in circles, rolling on her back, barking, and singing, "I just love my mom! I love my mom! I am okay and happy!"

She is doing well in the afterlife. She's happy. However, she does miss MAS and wants to make contact with MAS more often.

She is telling her person to listen for her when the wind is in the trees.

She is glad MAS is listening to her conversation. She's thankful that I am interpreting her voice for you. This conversation is extremely important for her.

Intuitive Wisdom Message from Charlie Girl to MAS

Trust your voice. Trust your inner voice. Trust your universal voice, and always trust the words that you choose to say. The words you choose for your soul, your heart, and for those around you.

Keep in mind that sometimes you might want to blurt out just like I did, and that that's okay, as there's no harm. This is a learning experience for us. We are teachers for each other in the physical life and in the afterlife.

I am with you. The rustle of the trees for the most part, but when you hear the wind whisper, I am there too.

When I came to you, I really needed a mentor and teacher. MAS, you gave that to me, and I'm forever ever thankful. I came into your life at an important time. I taught you and will continue to teach you frequently, if not everyday, to live your life trusting your inner voice.

I am asking you leave your heart open and always leave your heart open to the all the positive, intuitive things that come your way. There is an important lesson here.

First, be sure to listen to your intuition immediately and without haste. If a situation, person, thing, emotion, etc., feels positive, then open your heart. If it does not feel positive, do not open your heart yet. It is all about learning how to sharpen this skill.

I am a master of this. I can change energy quickly and make it positive and healthy.

Both of us have strong gifts for each other and a strong promise for each other. Our bond is quite beautiful. My biggest lesson and words of wisdom for you: never give up on yourself; never give up on your intuition.

You intuition is a powerful mechanism for allowing love, trust, and the world to guide you. Mom, I am your teacher and that will never end. Please listen to your intuition, as your intuition will change your world. Think of me as you're doing this, as you are practicing believing in yourself and believing in your wisdom.

You gave me the space, the safety, and the heart to trust in myself. I'm asking you to share your heart with peace and joy but never ever forget who you are inside. Instead, integrate yourself with your universal self, and you will feel complete.

Love in my heart,

Charlie Girl

Love Note to Charlie Girl from MAS

Dear Charlie Girl,

You have helped me on so many levels. You confirmed for me that I needed to trust my inner voice, my intuition. I often find this hard to do, but hearing this from you has given me the confidence to live my life trusting my inner voice.

I am so grateful to know that you are happy in the afterlife.

I know you will always be with me "in the rustle of the trees" and the "whisper of the wind."

Love,

MAS

Critical Insight

A significant message Charlie Girl communicated that we all need to pay careful attention to is:

Always pay attention to the words you choose to say to yourself and others.

7—Partnership in Healing

I can see you have done much work with shifting your energy system. You have gotten clear of things that were blocking you. You also have discovered new ways to respond to the world.

—Chris, the cat

Chris is a domestic, shorthair feline. He's 11, living, and was adopted.

Intuitive Conversation with Wendy

This is what Chris communicates at first: "Oh man ... do I have to talk? Don't you guys just get it? We, cats, especially me, just can't believe you aren't as enlightened as us. I know we need you. After all, we live with you and you feed us. I get that it is a nasty place out there in the world to be a feral cat. But honestly—I don't have time for this."

As I connect with Chris this is the way he first talks with me. I stop and I listen. I don't leave him. He tries to get me to leave, but I ask my Spirit Guides and his if it is okay to stay. They unanimously decide: YES stay ... He just needs time. He is grieving.

This is his shell and sometimes the way Chris sees new energy and new people. There is a part of his energy field that has not healed. This allows certain people, animas, events, issues, etc., to affect him.

Although he shows me a hardness, a distrust, and a "don't mess with me" attitude—he is a cat that is sweet and endearing. He is a great cat, and he appreciates that I am not pushing him.

I tell him to take all the time he needs to process what is going on. We are here to support him and give him the sacredness of this space.

He meows sweetly.

I tell him I will sit and wait until he is ready to have a conversation with us. Chris watches to see what I do. I relax and breathe. I allow him to search my energy field on his terms. I tell him this is about him.

Approximately five minutes pass …

Chris is now comfortable and open to talk. He tells me he is grieving still for his human dad. He is confused as to why this person left. He tells me something did not go well.

I explain to Chris that his human dad died. Chris knows this, but he needs help from CD, his person.

I also tell him that I can help him heal his energy discomfort. And he allows me. But there are steps CD must take as well.

Intuitive Wisdom Message from Chris to CD

I can now breathe. And I thank you for respecting me and having the desire to hear what I have to say. I haven't been able to talk and have anyone listen for quite a while.

I am sensitive. Just like you. We are sensitive on various levels. Not just on the physical, but mostly on the spiritual. I hope we can actively work on this together.

One thing I don't understand is why my dad died. It is important you told Wendy about this event. It is not by surprise or by chance you did so.

I know he died, and that is not what is confusing me. What is confusing me is that there was something off that day. And it left me with an energy hole I can't patch without your help. I can see you have one similar to mine. It will take some conscious effort and loving ways to heal our energy holes, but I am dedicated to working with you.

I would like you to go into meditation with me. I would like you to connect with my energy and our guides. I would like for you to become aware of what we can do together. This is not an idle request, and you may not be ready just yet. But know I have the patience to wait until you are ready to work on this.

I can see you have done much work with shifting your energy system around. You have gotten clear of things that were blocking you. You also have discovered new ways to respond to the world. But as you grow there will be more demands. I will be by your side as you are beside me.

You see, I came into your life to help you with contacting the animal kingdom. You have great skill in this way. We see you as a feline comrade and as an advocate for our feline voices.

You have taken many of us in, and you understand the feline energy system. But you haven't trusted or discovered that of your own yet. This I can help with. You see, I am your conduit. I am your learning bridge. I am here to help you with your skills. But it will take time and work to get there.

Our main and first goal now is to heal this energetic hole that we share. It is located on our right shoulders. Both of our energy holes originated from unresolved experiences of grief, namely abandonment.

Visualize yours, and I will visualize mine. Then we switch, and I visualize yours and you visualize mine.

I then need you to talk with me on an energy level and assure me that abandonment will not reoccur in my life in the same way. It is confusing to me. When my dad died, my energy became disjointed. I can't heal until I get the safety switch turned on again.

I know living things die, but the complexity of abandonment is what I don't understand. Once you explain that to me my energetic hole will heal and so will yours.

Remember, we are souls destined to work together in the realm of energetic animal physics. The blending of our visualizations, breathing, and time switching are our methods.

Respectfully and soulfully sacred,

Chris

PS—thank you for taking me in and for this conversation.

Love Note to Chris from CD

Dear Chris,

You words are important to me. They are clear and concise.

Thank you for reminding me that I am able to shift my energy system and clear things that are blocking me. Your wisdom message has allowed me to respond to the world in new ways.

Your promise that you will always be by my side is encouraging and reassuring.

Your partner,

CD

Critical Insight

An essential element of Chris's message, one that we should all consider, is:

Learn about what is keeping you from being happy, take a breath, and then move from that place.

8—Healing Hands in Stillness

Today I'm giving you the gift—the gift of how to settle your mind through connection with nature and me. I am giving you the gift of becoming aware of your healing hands.

—Coco, the dog

Coco is a living, 6-year-old, female beagle. She is not a rescue. This is one of two intuitive conversations between Coco and JS (the second appears in chapter 29).

Intuitive Conversation with Wendy

As I connect with Coco I can see energy both from a desire to do well and a wanting to be understood. Coco looks at me seriously and says, "I am happy too!"

Coco tells me that she has many facets to her personality, and at times she is shy about showing herself. This is not a negative thing by any means; it's just another part of Coco. She is showing me a lovable and endearing dog. She asks JS, her person, to help her feel more confident.

She asks that JS explain things more. She would like to hear about JS's day, life, thoughts, and feelings. She doesn't want baby talk. She is telling me she doesn't like baby talk. She loves to hear things in a normal tone.

I ask her if she never wants baby talk. She tells me it's okay when JS is being silly with her—but not for important things.

I'm seeing her energy as happy and resourceful. She's happy for many reasons; it doesn't come frivolously. But Coco adds that she can be really goofy happy too.

What I love about Coco is that she has a nice blend of smarts, seriousness, and playfulness. Energy is telling me she doesn't always let on about what she's doing, thinking, or planning.

She has an impish way about her, for sure.

Intuitive Wisdom Message from Coco to JS

I just have to tell you something, JS. I think you're great. I enjoy my life with you tremendously. I am here for some specific reasons for you—and you for me.

My number one reason for being here with you is companionship. I know that might seem obvious and expected. I offer you a sense of calmness whenever you may need it. And you do that for me too.

Keep in mind, our touch is important. Your hands are incredibly healing for you and me. When you touch me, I know the world is okay and you do too. You may not always be aware of this, but I can help you with it. If you feel overwhelmed, stressed, overly concerned, or worried—just touch me. Put your hand on my heart, my back, or my head, and the energy in your body will immediately switch over to balance.

I could teach you a lot. I want you to listen to your intuition when you put your hands on my body. Hear your thoughts and what the world around you is giving to you as a gift.

When we sit together in the beauty of nature, I encourage you to ask me questions or just be still and quiet. I like quiet. As you place your hands on my body and we relax together, this is our purpose.

In the stillness let's synchronize our breathing. Did you know dogs breathe intentionally? We think about it a lot. But it does come naturally to us too—more than for humans. Humans have forgotten the energy behind breathing. Yes, it keeps us alive, but it also is the conduit for connecting to the inner self. Breathing also helps us connect to our surroundings.

As you sit with me I would like you to put your hands on my body—not to massage—but just gently place your hands on my body. Feel the warmth on your palms, on your fingers, on your fingertips. Feel every single blade of my fur on your hands. And breathe with me. You can close your eyes and listen to the sounds of nature. Listen to all the sounds around and within you. Breathe calmness. Open your heart and feel the love that you have for yourself, for me, for others—for the world around you!

Let your body sink into the earth; calm your thoughts and your worries, so you can gracefully move through your day with greater awareness and strength.

You can see how strong and happy I am. You can also see how intentional I am too. All of this is important.

I came into your life because you asked me to. I came into your life because I wanted to become part of your life. You brought me into your life and are allowing me to be your teacher.

Today I'm giving you the gift of how to settle your mind through connection with nature and me. I am giving you the gift of being aware of your healing hands.

Because of you I am able to teach this to you. That is important for me. My goal for you is to help you become aware of and feel your intuition in order to take care of yourself and heal.

I am really glad we are together. I wouldn't have it any other way. Our destiny is to be together and help each other every single moment, every single day, whether we are physically together or apart.

I love the way we spend our days together.

I love you,

Coco

Love Note from JS to Coco

Dear Coco,

Thank you for your beautiful and amazing Animal Wisdom. I cried tears of joy and gratitude. I feel so blessed because of you.

Thank you for saving my life through a difficult year. As my wise teacher, I appreciate you reminding me to open my intuitive gifts.

Coco, we share a deep love and bond. I love you for prompting me to find the truth of who I am. I am grateful for you.

Namaste,

JS

Critical Insight

Coco imparts numerous words of wisdom. In particular let's notice this message:

Settling your mind will ease overload, stress, or worry. Take the time you need to settle your mind.

9—The Zen Master's Sunshine

*Be open to the feelings and emotions that are
transcribed in the moment.*

—Lilly, the cat

Lilly was a domestic, female, calico cat. She was a rescue, and
she died at 16 years old. She was in the afterlife when we
connected.

Intuitive Conversation with Wendy

I'm sensing from Lilly her great wisdom for everything in life.
She was a smart cat and still is. Her energy and personality
have a Zen master quality.

I am seeing her thoughtful, contemplating life. She basically
doesn't let anything get past her. Lilly is aware of her
surroundings. She's knowledgeable and accountable. She
expects that from everybody else around her, in a good way.

She has patience but also expresses impatience at times. She
was and still is a fair teacher. Lilly continues this role in the
afterlife.

Intuitive Wisdom Message from Lilly to LW

I bring to you great mastery from what I learned prior to my experience of the physical world with you. Keep in mind, it was with you that I could fine-tune these abilities.

We worked together in the physical, regulating and calculating the energy and choices around us. Not always easy, but we were successful. I know that. You know that.

I have much to thank you for. You helped me develop into a strong, reliable, intuitive, and masterful kitty. I came to you because you opened the universal energy portal to allow this to happen. It was divine intervention that we spent time together.

And here's the wonderful thing—I gave you the same. I came into your life to help you become stronger, more reliable, and masterful.

You are accomplishing this very well, but I would like you to trust your intuition and yourself more deeply. Honor yourself as I do—as a Zen master does. I would like you to trust those gut feelings that you have. Don't discount them, for they are real. When you listen to them, you will grow in a different way.

As the sun shines in your world I remind you: there is a portion of us in every ray of sun. We radiate warmth and energy, and it will be the sun that will feed and remind you of my presence.

When a surprising ray of sun hits your right shoulder, know that is me. Stop what you are doing and take a breath to absorb the warmth. Be open to the feelings and emotions that are transcribed in that moment.

If there is not an actual ray of sunshine, you can create one in your mind's eye. Have it be bright! Have it be warm! Picture it hitting you gently on your shoulder like a soft tap of memory. I am here—you are here. We are together always.

Don't delay in your growth. I learned from you to trust my wisdom, my inner knowledge, and my intuition when making any kind of choice.

It is because of you that I am the Zen kitty in the afterlife. I am being celebrated for doing such a wonderful job and learning much in the physical world. That is how I like to be known for now.

I know you do not delay with your growth. You're a wonderful person and have a wonderful heart. If I'd chosen anyone else in my last life, I wouldn't be as strong or insightful as I am now—and forever.

Know that I will be living in the afterlife for a while. I don't know how long. Know I'm okay with this because I am being celebrated in the afterlife. I am being recognized for how I helped you in the physical. I did my job. You allowed me to do my job and to help you on a deep level. I taught you to grow and become confident on a profound and deeper level.

I am here today to tell you, thank you for being a wonderful human. I appreciate the incredible life that you gave me.

This is important for us cats, when we go into the afterlife: to know we did our jobs for our people. To help them grow and learn. Many people don't learn this from cats, but you have.

My life's purpose was fulfilled because of you. You saved me, you loved me, and you cared for my wellbeing. And you let me be me, at my own pace.

As we continue to love and care for each other, I will live in your heart and soul. Remember, I will be there every time the sun shines on your right shoulder. We are forever souls together.

Shining brightly forever,

Lilly

Love Note to Lilly from LW

Dear Lilly,

Thank you for talking with me. Knowing you are okay in the afterlife has brought me a great sense of peace.

I learned so much from your Wisdom Message. This conversation has allowed my heart to heal, knowing we are forever connected with every ray of sunshine.

You have taught me to trust my intuition, which reinforces my confidence in trusting my gut decisions.

Knowing you are the sunshine in my world allows me to open my heart and grow.

Best regards,

LW

Critical Insight

Let's revisit Zen Master Lilly's sage words:

Your growth will continue when you trust your wisdom. Be aware of what is around you.

10—One Love Forever

Our hearts saved each other. Our intuitions taught each other. Our minds provided the support for each other. We helped each to be safe, supported, and loved. We are one love forever.

—Max, the cat

Max is a domestic, shorthair, male feline. His died at 11 years of age. He was a rescue. He was in the afterlife when we connected.

Intuitive Conversation with Wendy

Max shows me a resourceful cat. The energy is clear and colorful. He is very specific about his Wisdom Message for today.

Even though he proudly shows me all the colors of his energy projections, there are two for our communication session today—blue and purple.

According to Max, he wants his person, MB, to have the colors blue and purple with her at all times. Wear them often. Also, have blue and purple present in the living space.

He tells me he likes flowers.

He is adamantly reminding me he is feline and wants to be referred to as a cat or feline—not a kitty—when we converse. He also shares that even though he is adorable, he prefers to be considered handsome.

He knows what he wants and doesn't hesitate to ask for it. He is forthright, honest, fair, and deliberate. Max has great energy and a delight for conversation.

He is sharing this bit of information in order to deliver his precise message. He needs to be clear and concise. He tells me it is important for him to talk with MB. He wants MB to first listen carefully, deliberately, and mindfully. No rushing or attempting to predict the message. Trust the message as is and keep the wisdom simple in the soul. Do not complicate the messages he gives, as that will dilute its purpose.

Max has a 7-day plan for his person, MB, to work towards deeper awareness of both his presence and their shared presence.

Intuitive Wisdom Message from Max to MB

I would like to get right into our work today. You know I am direct. You know I am fair. You also know I am honest in my reactions to you. It is clear this message needs to be in your soul.

I am supplying you with a 7-day awareness plan. Each day there is a task along with a color for you to bring into your life. I will keep it easy for you, as I want you to experience the wholeness of it.

Yes, there is more than what I am sharing now, and it may take time for you to receive it all. You may need extra guidance to receive everything, but for today and the next seven days, here is your task.

This process will be unique for you. When you act, do so with my essence present. I am here always to guide you. It will be important for you to take your time and only do one day at a time. Please read one at a time, and then visualize the task in meditation.

Day 1: Hot Pink: Today's lesson is about oneness and knowingness. It's about the compassion I gave you and you gave me. It is about the harmonious and peaceful hearts that we shared together and about being nonreactive in our joined spiritual love.

Day 2: Purple with Sparkles: You already know by learning from me that intuitive choices for the greater good are your key to the subtle awareness of the two of us a whole. How do you move through the world? Be aware of this as you feel my gifts of trust and intuition.

Day 3: Vibrant Blue: When we spent our life together, I was forever supporting you with speaking up, releasing, and communicating. Do you remember that? Bring me back into our blue universe. Feel my life force strengthening your breathing and voice. Remember, you supported me with releasing and communicating.

Day 4: Grass Green: I feel you coping with the loss of me as well as of others. You bring so much to our hearts. Know I live with our harmony, trust, lovingness, and gentleness. Today feel how you gave, give, and receive. Be in the balance of the moment.

Day 5: Fire Yellow: My soul combined with your soul is perfect. Our mental connection helps each of us with our beliefs, thoughts, and security in our choices. In our gentleness you allowed me to come into your soul and help you feel the balance of your mind, and you did the same for me.

Day 6: Autumn Orange: Never feel as if you have to let go of joy, warmth, or trust to make the decisions in your life that challenge you. There is joy in the beginnings and endings. Yes, our physical life together ended. But we gave birth to a new spiritual relationship that could only occur from the feelings and emotional lessons we learned in the physical world together.

Day 7: Red Sand: Play and remember to physically feel the lightness of being. Ground that action into the sacred heart connection you and I have.

Remember: our hearts saved each other. Our intuition provided support for you to be the best human and for me to be safe, supported, and loved. We are one love forever.

Love,

Max

Love Note to Max from MB

Dear Max,

Thank you for your Wisdom Message where you devised an amazing color plan to assist me in developing our nonphysical connection.

I love how you instructed me to call you back in the "blue universe!"

Now, when out-of-the-blue, the song lyrics pop into my head, "You're just to good to be true—can't take my eyes off of you—

you'd be like heaven to touch..." I know we're "home" together.

Forever,

MB

Critical Insight

When Max reminds MB of the following, it serves as a significant message to all of us as well:

When you are honest with yourself, your mindfulness will be effortless

11—Clarity

Survey your world and let in what is healthy and real for you ONLY.

—Hampton, the dog

Hampton was a Brittany. He died when he was approximately 11 years of age. He was a rescue. He was in the spirit world when we connected.

Intuitive Conversation with Wendy

I am struck and privileged to share Hampton's purity, strength, wisdom, and energy. He is a teacher and projects realism, regalness, and Zen mastership.

He is calm, calculating, fair, and honest. His energy is delightfully serious and intelligent.

He tells me that in the physical, he watched his world seriously, took everything in, and enjoyed surveying his world. Hampton is a proud dog that enjoyed his life tremendously.

In the afterlife he is seen as a master and is a highly respected being. He shares with me that this is how he sees SF, his person—as a teacher and master. SF is someone who is highly respected in all that he does.

Hampton ushers all animals into the afterlife when they first arrive. It is an important job that he is proud of.

Intuitive Wisdom Message from Hampton to SF

I want to thank you for bringing me into your life. When I first saw you, I knew I was going to spend my life with an equal, someone as wise and as intelligent as me. I had an idea this would happen at some point. I wasn't sure when, but I learned quickly as soon as we connected. Suddenly it became clear to me.

When I first saw you, something happened in my heart. I knew you were going to give me the time, respect, and energy needed for me to develop into the teacher I am. This insight that I gained from you gets noticed here in the afterlife. I am quite celebrated here because of what I accomplished in the physical.

I am forever grateful to you for saving me. And I know I saved you too. That was our promise together—to save each other's hearts. I came into your life to teach you the realization that life is truly beautiful, safe, and great.

What I love about you is that you took the time to allow me to develop and gave me the space to be who I truly am. My gift to you is the same—to give you the space, patience, and intelligence to be who you are and feel good about that. To give yourself unconditional love that is critical for your soul.

This is your lesson. I am asking you to survey your world and let in what is healthy and real for you ONLY. Be proud of your creations and how you help the world.

I would like to remind you to not judge your heart. Your heart is solid. It's love. Your heart knows. It's your intuition, which is also your center.

There is much judgment in this world. But together, our energies are clear and pure. Trust this. Trust it as you move forward every day in your personal quest for truth.

You can talk to me. Take my photograph and look into my eyes. Take a breath and ask me what you want to know. Ask me to keep you strong. Ask me how my lessons can guide you now. It's okay to do this. It is not weird because this is how our energy works together. When our energy is in sync, I will help you with difficult decisions and people, and help strengthen the unconditional nature of our love together.

You know, we do give unconditionally already together. Together we know how important our message is to those around us. There is more for you to learn, and my goal is to continue to teach you. And I think you already understand this. In fact—I know you understand this already.

I ask you to be patient with yourself and what you learn in life. You were patient and loving with me. I would like to remind you to do the same for yourself. I'm here to support you always. All you have to do is think about me. I will be there for you, and I will never ever leave you.

Know this is not an easy thing to do, but with our gratitude it will stream within its course. Stay patient, and trust what comes to you. Do know that your potential is still growing?

There's also something to be said about the sounds of nature and how our various connections with each other come forth. I'm sending you breeze—the breeze in the trees. Listen to the sounds and allow the messages you feel to come to you. Also sounds of water are another way to make connections with me in nature.

Don't forget who you are, what you do, and your amazing soul, heart, and intelligence.

Through your clarity you give people clarity. Remember how clear I was in the physical when I was given the choice. This clarity is my appreciation of you. Be aware of this and go to the place in your heart where we live together—always.

Calmness is also important for you. Remember to think about the air you breath and how this air will be part of me coming to you—to calm you when needed. We make our connections with nature—not only the trees and the water but with the air itself.

We will continue to join our hearts and teach from our place of knowing and intuition. Remember this always.

Love and appreciativeness,

Hampton

Love Note to Hampton from SF

Dear Hampton,

Your Wisdom Message came at a time when I really needed it. Before your death you were my constant companion. I loved our hiking, mountain biking, and snowshoeing adventures because you were a great listener while I sorted out aspects of my daily life.

Having the opportunity to reconnect with your spirit and hear your wise words once again was a gift beyond measure.

As I face a recent diagnosis of breast cancer and the treatment that will come along with that, I am happy to have your words to revisit again and again.

Your words remind me to get out and walk in the woods, to reconnect with the breeze in the trees and sounds of water, and to breathe in the air. They will be important aspects of my healing.

I cherish the thought knowing that your healing energy will be with me as I embark on my journey. I know in my heart I will regain my health. I will one day look back on this as just one little blip on my timeline.

Thank you,

SF

Critical Insight

It's very meaningful to all of us when Hampton points out:

Remember to give yourself the space, patience, and intelligence to be who you are and feel good about that.

12—The Heart's Wild Calm

Hear my whispers in the wind. I am calling you. Howl at the moon with me. It's okay, and it's cleansing for you to do so.

—Zorah, the dog

Zorah is deceased. She was a Siberian Husky rescue. She was approximately 10 when she died. She was in the afterlife when we connected.

Intuitive Conversation with Wendy

As I connect in with Zorah she shows me her deep and profound connection to the wilds of her being, of her soul, and to the wilds in which her soul lives on.

She has incredible light coming from all aspects of her soul force. Zorah is powerful, insightful, calm, and intelligent. Her energy centers are brilliant. She tells me she is about light and healing now. She also tells me she is about reminders and accountability. She is not lost, but active, healthy, and mentoring many.

Her work for her person, MW, is about self-discovery by exploring the wilds of the heart. She is willing to explore that with MW. In order to do this MW must ask her and accept what comes in as truth. Not to be questioned.

I ask her about MW's connection to Alaska. She explains that it's time for MW to discover the wilds of her heart. Alaska represents that. Zorah stresses the importance of MW trusting her wild side without adding challenging questions. "Try and be spontaneous but to survive and thrive—be careful not overdo it and drain yourself." The wild is the reflection from Zorah's light to MW's.

Intuitive Wisdom Message from Zorah to MW

I hear your soul calling. I hear your heart calling me. Why question? Why doubt? There is no need for that anymore.

Your strength is within your DNA, and your light is within mine. There is nothing to worry about anymore. There is nothing that can penetrate that sense of being-ness. I am here to be with you and to keep you safe.

Hear my whispers in the wind. I am calling you. Howl at the moon with me. Its okay, and it is cleansing for you to do so.

I have your back, as always, and I am not far from you, ever. I know you have challenges, but what human doesn't?

Keep in mind, you are connected to the spirit world already. Be present for the quiet whispers and messages in the wind and in your dreams. Be open to them, but do not demand or expect them to be obvious.

When clouds drift over you, that's my sign for you to take some time out for yourself. I ask you to connect with me when this happens. Just ask me to come and then look into my eyes. I will give you the answers. Please trust that. Don't be frustrated if perfection is not reached. I am here. I am the clouds and the whisper of their voices.

Our bond is unique and treasured by me. I will always be grateful for the rescue and bringing me into your home. Do know that this was divine intervention? This was the plan. I asked for you and you came to me.

You asked for me too. I heard your words and came your way. You needed me to remind you to listen to your heart, and I needed a human to give me the respect, compassion, and intelligence to be the teacher I was meant to be in the physical. You did this for me. Thank you.

The biggest gift I can give you today is calmness of heart: the breath of our souls melting and intertwining to form a single energy force and creating love.

This love is for you only. I see you give out love and compassion at the expense of your own health. Be aware of this. Love yourself first, and then check in to see if there is any to give to others.

You do not travel alone. You have many that support you. Your Spirit Team is secure within your space and environment. There are others as well; ask them to come forth. It doesn't matter what they look like or what they do for you; just ask them to help and they will be there.

I have much to be grateful for here in the afterlife. Being in the form of energy is not much different from when I was in the physical on earth. A husky is always connected to both the physical and spiritual. We are pure... We are ancient. Our spiritual-ness is unadulterated.

I would like to ask you to always manage your energy—never forget that. Be pure as a husky and find great connection by tuning in to your inner wildness.

Alaska is your place of wildness and your home. Be there. Go there … in any way you can.

Wild calmness,

Zorah

Love Note to Zorah from MW

Dear Zorah,

Your Wisdom Message for me was so like you. I thank you for being a wonderfully happy husky.

You always wanted to please me and have fun in every way. Our special bond comes through clearly in your message to me. You taught me the powerful meaning of love, spiritualness, and energy.

Thank you, Zorah, you are special, and you'll always be in my heart.

From the wildness of my heart,

MW

Critical Insight

Zorah supports all of us, particularly when she tells MW:

Trust your wild side. Be spontaneous to survive and thrive. Howl at the moon!

13—Thirteen Lives to Fulfillment

*Look at what I have been through—feel me—
know and trust what I'm telling you is true—I am
your teacher. I am here as your guide to help you
discover and sharpen the promise that you have
been destined to sign with me.*

—Oliver, the cat

Oliver is 13 years of age and a domestic, shorthair cat. He was found outside a nursing home. He's living.

Intuitive Conversation with Wendy

Oliver wants us to know that being abandoned was just part of his journey. We should not be overly concerned, but be aware and come back to this concept at times ourselves.

He is not stressed out about it. He tells me that this was just part of his particular spiritual plan. His promise was to learn and then teach.

But my Spirit Team and that of his person, CD, are saying we need to look at abandonment more because there is a lesson there for CD in particular.

I love his matter-of-factness. He's not about drama or about victimhood. He knows himself well. This was partly because of his Soul Promise to deal with victimhood and abandonment.

Oliver shares, "Even though my mom mentioned I was abandoned three times before in previous lives, there are many more than that! In fact, please tell her it was 12 times."

Each time Oliver was abandoned, there was a new part of his promise to discover and incorporate into his soul, a promise he'll soon explain. He is methodical, purposeful, and dutiful. It took him 12 rounds (this being the thirteenth). The divine plan for him was to not complete his promises quickly. For each lifetime the thread was the same. The thread was about gaining trust in oneself and gaining the strength needed for many different challenges in life. Oliver was presented with some incredible lessons during these lives. Unfortunately, or fortunately, depending how you want to look at it, it took him a long time to gain trust and strength within himself.

Oliver tells me that this is not a negative thing. He doesn't want CD to feel sorry for him or wish his life was different because it is/was perfect. He understands that the universal force had a divine plan for him and has one for CD.

Intuitive Wisdom Message from Oliver to CD

If I didn't need thirteen lives to pick families or situations to test my abilities to become strong and trusting, I would've never come to the physical world to you—this thirteenth time.

I heard you when you were ready to come into this physical world. You asked for a particular cat to help you. I came forth and promised to walk with you on your journey that included dealing with feeling alone and the perception of being totally misunderstood by everyone. This is our shared path for healing each other.

Keep in mind, you are not abandoned in this way—your heart was never lost. You may feel so at times. You may feel alone and feel like things are against you. Remember, I agreed to work with you at the perfect time.

It doesn't matter now how many times you or I feel left alone or when this was the truth for us. What matters is we become aware and accountable for each other and our own selves. We see the positive. [Note from Wendy: Oliver is saying this loudly.]

The past is not important anymore. I know that I have finally learned what I have been destined to learn. I have gained trust, security, and strength.

I am not sure you totally understand this yet for yourself. But if you can look at what I have been through, you will know and trust that what I'm telling you is true.

I am here as your teacher. I am here as your guide to help you discover and fine-tune the promise you have been destined to sign with me. I am here to remind you to look, recognize, and embrace your inner strength—always.

Take care of yourself. Remember to look at me. I'm a survivor and so are you. It doesn't matter how many times you have to go through things to learn a lesson. We are not counting here. This is not a race or a contest. This journey is not about anyone—but you and me.

Remember, I came into being this thirteenth time FOR YOU! I am here to warm your inner soul and to keep you on track.

Sometimes you forget to stay on track. You get flustered and stop believing in yourself.

I am kind and gentle, but I'm also serious. I'm important to you, and I will continue to remind you: do not get quiet about your journey.

Do you see those marks above my eyes, in between my ears? Those are symbols for you to remember. You can gaze into those marks when you're feeling unsure, lost, and alone in your beliefs, or when you're feeling like no one gets you! Just look into those shapes and allow them to encompass your soul and your aura.

Remember to bring these shapes behind and in front of you, to your sides, on the bottom of your feet, and on the top of your head. Let these shapes encompass your entire world being on the external, and bring them into your heart.

CD, your journey is perfect. Don't delay. Don't doubt—you are perfect.

Perfectly yours,

Oliver

Love Note to Oliver from CD

Dear Oliver,

I will trust you as my teacher. You have offered me trust, security, and strength.

Trust has always been difficult for me, but I am committed to personal growth in this area. I am working on trusting myself to gain the strength needed for many of life's challenges.

In mindful strength,

CD

Critical Insight

Oliver delivered many powerful insights. One that is so relevant to all of us that we should refer to often is the following:

It doesn't matter how many times you have to go through things to learn a lesson. This part of your journey is not about anyone—but you!

14—Grace and Gratitude

Together we are beautiful and kind. We show the world many great things.

—Randy, the dog

Randy was a male Maltese-Australian Silky Terrier cross. He was 16 when he died. Randy was a rescue. He was in the spirit world when we connected.

Intuitive Conversation with Wendy

Randy is a dear and loving soul. His energy is quiet. He's in a place of calmness, perception, and solace. He's showing me that all is good in his world now.

He shares with me that there's also a little confusion. He says it's not a bad thing, and he knows it will become clear soon.

He's wondering what I am doing here. He wasn't expecting any visitors today. He looks up at me and smiles. He questions me with kindness.

I tell him that I'm here to talk to him and his person, CT, would like to hear his Wisdom Message.

As soon as I told him that CT wanted to hear from him his entire energy shifted. He went from quiet and resourceful to gleefully goofy.

He is going in circles, barking, and carrying on—extremely happy. He is exclaiming, "This is great! This is great! This is great! I can't wait—this is great!" [I can't help but giggle.]

I ask him if he is ready to give CT a Wisdom Message, and he, of course, replies, "YES!"

Intuitive Wisdom Message from Randy to CT

Even though I have been away for a long time from the physical, I would like to remind you I do come and visit you often.

I hear you when you think about me. I hear you all the time when you think about me. You may not know that, but I do. We are close in our energy connection—forever.

The gratitude that I feel for you is forever. The grief that you feel is your love for me. Your grief is kind and loving. It's real and appreciated. Your gratitude for me is perfect and will be forever—never to be lost.

What I can tell you is that life is decisive. Yes, it has mystery and drama. I hope this will help you with your daily living as I continue to share.

Life isn't all that difficult. Humans tend to feel like it is, but it's really about life being decisive. This is simple, really.

What does this mean? As you think of me and I hear you, our energy bodies immediately connect. Our energy bonds together. Life can become easier.

The past doesn't really matter. It's what we're doing now. When our energies combine while you are thinking of me, that's what starts all the forward motion of making decisions in life. The motion is set into being and committed to going forward.

When you need to make a difficult decision, consider it a good thing. Think of me, and I will help you. Our energy will connect, and I WILL help you make the decision. Trust this and remember, I can see what is happening and can help you be decisive.

As you open your heart to this possibility your world will become easier—larger. Your world will become softer. Yes, I know you can make good decisions. I've seen you do that, but this is going to make it even better. It is going to balance you even more.

I think about you a lot and come to check up on you many times throughout the days. Nothing is planned. It is when the energy is open for doing so on my end. But I am always there when you think of me.

The love between us is full of our gratitude for life and for the decisiveness that life has for us. I am grateful for you.

It's not always about making decisions but about taking life as clear and clean as it is. People tend to dilute things, confuse things, and make things more difficult. Don't you think?

The decisive thing—the decisiveness of life—really doesn't have to be that decisive; it just is.

Keep moving forward, Mom, with the gratitude we share for each other. With that in mind your grace and heart will shine. Together we are beautiful and kind. We show the world many great things. I know you are the best because I witness that every day.

I haven't forgotten you, and I appreciate all that we shared and still share. You have given me the gift of trust, gratitude, and awareness. My gift to you is the same through seeing life as clear with many lessons along the way.

I miss you in the physical, but I am not far.

Love,

Randy

Love Note to Randy from CT

Dear Randy,

You were my first dog, and you showed me how special love is for us. I miss you, and I'm grateful for having you in my life.

I am glad you know I still think of you. You were my little mate as we shared many major changes in my life.

Thank you for continuing to still be there for me, and I will think of you when I have a difficult decision to make. Thank you for continuing to help me.

With gratitude,

CT

Critical Insight

An insight Randy makes that resonates with so many of us is:

Life is decisive. Yet, it has mystery and drama. See life with many lessons along the way.

15—Clearing the Space

*Allow for all the goodness that is meant for you,
just you! Allow yourself to come into the clear
space that you created.*

—Julie Mae, the cat

Julie Mae is an 18-year-old a rescue cat with a tortoiseshell coat. She is living.

Intuitive Conversation with Wendy

Julie Mae comes to me quietly, slowly, and deliberately. She is not in a rush, but she is curious and highly intellectual. She looks me straight in the eye. She offers full trust and transparency. She sees camaraderie in our connection.

Julie Mae loves to "play" with spiritual and mind energy. She finds it relaxing and healing.

Julie Mae is not only a Zen master but a healer as well. She excels in energy healings of the mind, brain, and skull. She has medical intuitiveness too. Julie Mae is an amazing feline.

It's lovely how trusting she is right from the beginning. She's actually now on my lap getting ready to climb up my arm and cuddle her head into my neck.

She tells me everything is okay and humans worry too much. Humans would be better off if they emulated cats more.

I ask her, "Why not dogs?"

She looks at me, responding, "Seriously, did you really just ask me that?"

Julie Mae is a cat to not fool around with. She is kind and gentle, but her words are wise, precise, and honest. Listen to her and do what she says. Each word is carefully calculated before she expresses herself.

Her energy is more of the mind and spiritual healing for her person, CA. She is here for her person and willing to help.

She mentions she's glad she's with CA because CA has given her the opportunity to heal herself, so she can help others.

She works with the spiritual world all the time.

Intuitive Wisdom from Julie Mae to CA

I speak with you today on even ground: peer to peer, knowledge to knowledge, and soul to soul.

It is no mistake I'm in your life. I want to thank you for taking me into your home and heart, but most of all into your entire mind. I'm appreciative of this gift, which I respect and enjoy.

There is something I would like you to do. I would like you to open your mind to something different today. Trust in the nature of the world, your world, and your surroundings. This will support you as you listen and hear what I have to say. It might be difficult for you at first. That's okay. There's no rush, but for the long term this is your task to become a better human and be calm with yourself.

One way to calm your mind when your thoughts are stirring is to sit quietly as I do. Observe and copy me. Watch my breath, body posture, and eyes. Try and connect with your mind, the way I do.

It will take practice and attention. As soon as you begin to feel stressful, question yourself. Stop! Stop what you are engaged in and do something else. It won't work if you try and push. Humans try and push for things to happen.

If you push, you will make yourself feel uneasy. The goal is for your mind to melt into your inner spirit, so you feel like the world is easier. This is the way cats think, you know.

Pushing is not good for you. It disrupts your unique flow, and your mind shuts down to your gifts of possibility. This is the way for you to come into and discover the purpose of your soul in a healthier way.

You helped me do this for myself. This is why we are together. First, you helped me, and now I am here to help you. I hope you give me this opportunity more.

The way to do this is to keep observing me. Keep watching me. Do as I do with my daily chores and rounds. Be precise but gentle with yourself. You taught me to be this way with myself.

Once you feel as if you are ready and you can calm the pounding of your mind and thoughts, please feel at peace with yourself and your surroundings.

Then visualize your mind opening to the sky. Gently. See the white and blue light. Feel the quiet breeze that cleanses your mind of all that stresses you. This breeze will take these thoughts and return them healthy and clear to their original home.

Then allow for all the goodness that is meant for you, just you, to come into this clear space in which you created. All the thoughts that stress you have left, and the only place for your mind to go is into the healing place. This will feel remarkable to you.

With deepest respect,

Julie Mae

Love Note to Julie Mae from CA

Dear Julie Mae,

You are so very wise. As I listen to your voice, connect with your energy, and practice what you recommend—it is absolutely astounding!

For the last several months in particular I have been having difficulty being kind to myself, and therefore, I have been feeling a lot of chaos and unsettledness. You remind me in a straightforward way what I need to do to feel good about myself.

Thank you for beginning to sleep with me at night, and for seeking me out for loving talk and touching.

Lovingly yours,

CA

Critical Insight

A resounding message for all of us to heed from Julie Mae is:

When you choose to open your mind, remember it will take time and patience. Be kind to yourself.

16—Bliss through Awareness

What is the meaning of bliss? It is not some vacuum or some airy-fairy concept. Bliss is cellular motion in the present time.

—Axle, the dog

Axle is a male Brittany who died at 14 years old. He was not a rescue. He was in the afterlife when we connected.

Intuitive Conversation with Wendy

Even though Axle was not a rescue dog, he shares, "What do you mean, 'not a rescue'? I *am* a rescue dog!"

After I explain to him that he was not a rescue dog and that SF was his person, he looks at me and again insists he was a rescue dog. I let this part of the conversation be for a while as an important part of our connection is to respect his translation of himself and to have time to clarify and even it out.

As Axle and I continue to connect he shows me light, laughter, ease, happiness, and warmth. His blue-violet light is regal and beautiful. He is heart and crown chakra-oriented.

As the "rescue" energy evens out and begins to settle it becomes clearer. It is apparent I needed to give Axle the space to share why he was saying this. I let him take his time with it.

Approximately eight minutes later, he begins to tell me he is not a rescued dog but a rescue dog. *He* does the rescuing.

He begins to show me a blissful nature within his soul. It's more than a simple happiness—a complete compatibility with his life in the physical as well as in the afterlife, a state of mind that contains energy, colors, and vibrations that filter and integrate throughout his body.

He shows me how important it is/was for him to be placed in SF's home where he could live and embrace his peace.

He appreciates everything he had and has now. He is aware of much and all. Axle's energy flies and floats. His energy is not much different in the afterlife as it was in his physical.

He is at peace. In fact, he never mentions any stress to me. My guides show me he is the representative for BLISS!

Intuitive Wisdom Message from Axle to SF

Did you know that bliss is the world for you and me? It is the inner baseline from which we travel apart and together. Bliss is my world as well as yours. Please think about this slowly. Please feel your bliss as my gift and its awareness towards healing.

This is not difficult for you to feel. It's really not hard at all when you think about it. Keep in mind that you have to be more dog-like with your thoughts when you consider bliss.

Think from a dog's perspective instead of a human's: what is the meaning of bliss? It is not some vacuum or some airy-fairy concept. Bliss is cellular motion in the present time.

When I watch you, I see that you are sometimes too invested in your human-ness. I feel for you when you are going through this. I know you understand bliss and what I am saying to you. I am asking you to discover the window of your bliss in a different way.

I know you feel this and are able to call upon the bliss of your nature and inner ecosystem. Bliss is not an outside force; instead, it's the base from which we grow and move.

Please allow your heart to shine and call upon your happiness when you feel blocked or when your energy is not moving, as you would like.

You have the tendency to absorb much of the energy around you. You forget to buffer your energy, and all of a sudden you feel as if you have been sideswiped. Sometimes you wonder why you are feeling like you do. This is because you are not fully connected to your inner bliss and your base.

My gift to you is to pour this delight into each cell, membrane, and energy container that you have. Explore these energy containers. Take a look at them and ask them what they need to be able to fill, with the result being bliss.

Now don't get bliss confused with lack of awareness and lack of feeling responsible—that's not what I am talking about.

Instead, let's look at how we can fill your breath, heart, cells, membranes, and all that encompasses any living being— namely you—with that underlying measure of bliss.

Let's do this together! Whatever action, thought, or feeling you have, keep in mind, it's based on your harmony.

Together let's feel the breeze of our world,

Axle

Love Note to Axle from SF

Dear Axle,

I am so glad that your spirit is blissfully happy. It warms my heart to know you are at peace.

I am struck that you call yourself a rescue dog, and I know exactly what you mean. We spent countless hours walking in the woods, not only enjoying nature but also using that time, using that peace and quiet to be introspective.

In a sense, this special time with you served to rescue me from a completely stressful worklife and served as a catalyst to some upcoming changes in my life.

You will always have a special place in my heart. Your wisdom reminds me to fully appreciate and understand the state of bliss to be found from within.

Blissfully Yours,

SF

Critical Insight

When Axle reminds SF of the following, it acts as profound message to all of us as well:

When you allow bliss to travel to your heart and soul, it then becomes part of who you are.

17—The Art of Limitless Change

Watch me as I walk through my space. I stop, I listen, I choose. I then move on. I decide what I take with me. No one else does.

—Myrtle, the cat

Myrtle is a tortoiseshell, female feline. She is a rescue and is estimated to be 13 years old.

Intuitive Conversation with Wendy

As I connect in with Myrtle she brings me to her spiritual place. It is not a place she shares with everyone. But she feels enlightened and calm there. She tells me it's her place where she ponders and discovers the world. She shares that it's always new and it provides exciting thoughts.

She tells me even at the age of 13 there are always new and exciting things to discover in her special place. This special place is where she goes when she connects to her spiritual side. She is inviting her person, CA, to visit her there. I tell her we can do this when she shares her Intuitive Wisdom.

Myrtle whispers to me that she's ancient and an old soul. I ask her why she is whispering. She tells me that she doesn't want the others to know. When I ask her who that is, she responds, "The other cats in my household."

She tells me she was brought to the physical to wander. She shows me this wandering is taking place with her thoughts and development through spiritual lessons.

It's important for her to add that energy is not random or needless pondering. Energy is deliberate, current, and apparent for things to be in balance.

Myrtle is a caretaker, to say the least. She is responsible for both her person and others. She tells me she watches over the other cats. In fact, all cats.

Myrtle tells me the other cats aren't as useful or as smart as she is. Her confidence and sassiness are apparent as we talk together.

I ask her if she has a Wisdom Message for CA, and she does.

Intuitive Wisdom Message from Myrtle to CA

My name is Myrtle. It is an interesting name, not one that I truly identify with. It's a name that really isn't one that I would choose for myself, but I can see why someone would name me this. It is an old name in the human world, and I am an old being.

I see myself more as an Ariel or Ariela. Call me this when you want to connect with me on an energetic and spiritual level.

I would like to share something that has to do with word/name choices. What I have discovered: names and labels of things do not matter. It's how you and I view the entire world and where we are placed in it that matters.

My hope is you will spend non-judgmental time pondering what I say. Please wander through your thoughts, and decide how to create the healthiest way to proceed in your daily world.

You see, this comes easy for me, as I am the gatherer. I have the ability to combine all energies to make something that works for the betterment of a single self. I try and do it for the other cats, and they often do well because they are healers too. But sometimes they miss the mark.

Let your mind wander and allow it to go to the places in your body where you may place limitations on yourself. Those limiting thoughts affect what you're thinking, how you communicate to others, and how you communicate to others about others.

Humans are an interesting yet complicated bunch. I have done a lot of studying—watching humans as they struggle with judgments, labels, opinions, and names. It seems to me if you let things wander on by and not try and hold onto things that don't matter, then your life could be filled with discoveries. Wonderful choices would be made with confidence, without drama, and the mind chaos that rules your daily life would literally fly away. I have seen it so many times, and it just fascinates me.

I would like to encourage you to be more like me when it comes to living your life. Watch me as I walk through my space. I stop, I listen, I choose. I then move on. I decide what I take with me. No one else does. My job is to help you move through your limitations with courageous effort. It really is up to you.

My heart to yours,

Ariel (formerly Myrtle)

Love Note to Ariel (formerly Myrtle) from CA

Dear Ariel,

At your request your name is now Ariel, not Myrtle. I love how you jumped into my arms, gave me kisses, and purred when I called you Ariel for the first time.

You are a gem—always present when I eat meals, then waiting until I finish to come close for conversation and petting. As you purr and snuggle I have learned to know your feelings and what you need.

I know you long for me to place limits on my work, so I have plenty of time for the spiritual side of life. Thank you for recognizing this and reminding me to take a needed break.

I also appreciate your reminders to be gentle with myself and allow my spirit to regroup and then soar with kindness.

With love,

CA

Critical Insight

Something Ariel says that we should all ponder is the following:

Limiting thoughts will affect your daily life. Moving through these types of thoughts will create courage.

18—Eyes: Love's Reflection

Please look into my eyes and see the love for your own heart. My eyes are your tools for healing.

—Sally, the cat

Sally is 2 years old and is a rescue. She is a common domestic feline with medium-long hair. She is living.

Intuitive Conversation with Wendy

Sally has strong feminine energy. She is sweet and soft. As she meows gently she crawls up into my lap and puts her paws on my chest. She looks deep into my eyes as we communicate together.

Sally is a visual cat. She shows me clearly what and how she wants to communicate with her person, MW.

Her energy is clear, clean, and pristine. She tells me she doesn't have time to spend on the more earthly stuff.

Sally is profound for one so young. She is still learning and growing. Yet she is being guided well.

She goes about her day seeing the goodness in life and isn't too upset by things.

She has nice energy. Kind energy. Young energy, but she is clear. She tells me she is still figuring things out and gets a little shaken at times. But once she stops trying so hard, she figures it out.

She shows me this is important for MW too. She would like MW to not only show her things MW would like her to do, but to explain them to her with easy steps and directions. She also tells me it is important for MW to change her own direction and be gentler on herself.

Sally wants to always be a good kitty. She wants to please her person. She never wants MW to be upset with her.

She tells me she likes to be near MW. In fact, she knows where MW is at all times. This makes her feel good.

She watches her person and keeps the energy around her person clean and clear. She is still working on this talent, but she is excited because she came to her person, so she could work on this task.

My Spirit Team tells me that Sally is doing well. The blunders are learning tools and reminders for MW to connect with Sally on a different level by explaining things step-by-step. This will help MW too.

Intuitive Message from Sally to MW

Please look into my eyes and see the love for your own heart. My eyes are your tools for yourself. I am here to help you with this. I am here to help you reflect back the love you have for yourself.

I came to you because of your heart. You came to me because of my heart. You have a generous heart, as do I. We made a promise to help each other trust our hearts for self-love. It is important for me to have a human that has this trait, and I am glad I picked you.

As you look into my eyes and see the love I have for you this reflects into your love for yourself. Do you know what I mean? It takes practice but no need to try too hard.

Please don't let your love for your beautiful soul ever fade. Please don't discount the validity of your heart connection to others.

Remember, your self-love is important first. Give the generous love you have to yourself first, and only then move from connecting to your own heart intuitively by giving it to others. This way you will stay healthy and strong. You will not feel drained or surprised by your decisions. This is a big task coming from such a young kitty, but these words are truth from me to you.

When you give to others first, without giving love to your own heart, your own intuition and choices may lead you down a more difficult path. This is okay and will be your destiny at times. But even during the difficulty, you can find your way into your own self-loving heart by looking into my eyes.

I am here to remind you, a difficult path is not always necessary. Sometimes you can be easy on yourself and hear your inner song of joy, peace, and being, feeling complete with who you are.

Now is time and time is now. Look into my eyes when you want to be cleared and reminded of the beauty of your soul, heart, mind, spirit, and body. Your Spirit Team guides and I are here to walk with you and never let you down.

I may be a young kitty, but I am wise for my age. I am learning so much from you and watching you. I am here as your teacher and mentor. Please ask me. Please talk with me as you are now.

Love,

Sally

Love Note to Sally from MW

Dear Sally,

I was positively relieved when I got your Animal Wisdom Message because I was worried how unfriendly you were ever since I got you. I was worried that I caused injury or you didn't like our place. From the moment I asked Wendy for a message from you, I saw how your behavior changed. You became more loving and attentive.

Loving you calmly,

MW

Critical Insight

Sally guides her person with many powerful insights. One, in particular, for us to reflect on is:

Give generous love to yourself first. When done mindfully, you are then able to give to others with compassion.

19—Profound Strength through Abandonment

*When you don't recognize your feelings of loss,
that part of our soul that we share is not engaged.*
—Baby, the cat

Baby is a deceased, domestic, shorthaired, orange tabby. He passed at the age of 11. He was adopted from a shelter.

Intuitive Conversation with Wendy

As I connect in with Baby he brings me to a place of abandonment. The general feeling is warmth, but there is also surprise. He shows me that even in his latest experience of abandonment, he felt like everything was going to be okay.

He tells me there were many life lessons for him to learn from his abandonment time to share with his person, MB. He wants MB to revisit with him feelings of abandonment for deep healing.

He is also sharing that even though his latest abandonment wasn't that traumatic, the experience still provided him with a lesson in life that was directed by the universe. This was a surprise to him. It came sooner than he'd expected.

Because he had been abandoned before in his previous lives, this time around it didn't need to be strong, forceful, or hugely traumatic. The purpose of that most recent abandonment was for him to fine-tune himself and then come into his person's life to help them with all that he experienced.

He and MB both made a Soul Promise to guide, help, and respect each other with great compassion with all types of loss and grief.

This promise actually occurred prior to MB's birth. Actually, at the time of MB's birth MB asked the universe to send a cat to help her learn and embrace her own feelings of loss. MB wanted to learn in this life how to find her place, wisdom, and confidence with self-appreciation and respect. To learn and heal from her losses.

He tells me he deeply respects his person and thanks her for opening up the universal channels for not only his healing but for allowing him to teach her.

Intuitive Wisdom Message from Baby to MB

Our calling for each other is profound, to say the least. I heard you calling within the universal confines of our connection prior to your birth—although I was not yet ready to join you in the physical and not ready to come forth to help you. Know I never lost sight of you at that time. I came quickly and connected with you when I heard you ask for me to come forth again.

We promised to join at the time of my re-emergence into my final physical place of learning. This was my time for becoming my own Zen master and yours.

I came to you when I was gently abandoned. It wasn't a horrible experience for me. I was fully aware. I knew what was happening as I asked to have this experience one more time, with you as the healer. I knew you were coming.

I came to you at a time in your life when you were ready to move forward with your own sense of loss, ready to recognize how the losses in life can actually help the individual to see beauty more deeply in life, and be ready to experience how loss can build strength from a unique place within.

Let's breathe together as we explore and connect our souls through our eyes of understanding.

Here is how it works: you know the feeling inside your body when you lose something of great importance? For instance, that feeling you had when I died? Your heart felt raw. You felt as if part of you was gone and never to return. That is how it feels as an animal when we are left, when we are abandoned. No matter if we have other animals around or not—rawness is there. Foster parents or not—rawness is present. There is a part of our soul that goes unrecognized for a while as we search for our Soul Promise mate. Sometimes this happens but sometimes not.

The same happens to humans. You can wander through your days, wondering how to get to the next moment after a loss. But when you have a Soul Promise mate, it can help lessons go a little smoother.

Our journey is to share, and I can still guide you here in the afterlife. I watch you everyday.

I would like to share with you this special and unique observation I have made of you from here in the afterlife ...

When you don't recognize your feelings of loss, that part of our soul that we share is not engaged. What happens next is your experienced loss, whether new or old, will not have the strength to ask for help. That's okay, but please remember to call upon me to guide you and connect with you. I want to continue to help your growth towards self-respect and mutual confidence as you did for me. Try not to give into being challenged by being unrecognized. Avoid being buried so deep you may forget why you are feeling the way you do.

I am here always,

Baby

Love Note to Baby from MB

Dear Baby,

When you were dying, I was terrified and knew I would feel horrible without you. Then when you died, my anxiety from the lack of your presence was overwhelming.

In your Wisdom Message the peace I feel now is indescribable. I now know you watch me every day and are guiding me on our joined path to Zen-hood.

Your messages to me are amazing. Thank you for guarding me while I sleep.

Mutual love,

MB

Critical Insight

Give additional attention to this aspect of Baby's message:

Losses can actually help you see the beauty more deeply in life.

20—Balance with Joy

*From the past we can garner the lessons of joy,
love, hope, and wisdom.*

—Oscar, the dog

Oscar is alive, and he's a mix-breed male. He's originally from Romania and is 2 years old.

Intuitive Conversation with Wendy

Oscar is wonderful. Bear and eagle energy come through as soon as I connect with his and my Spirit Teams.

He connects with his earthiness and sense of survival with the pace of a bear: slow, methodical, and feeling the earth with his paws.

He also communicates with the eagle spirits. Oscar surveys his world with an all-knowing sense. Knowing what is around, above, and beneath him at all times is important and necessary.

He is an aware puppy. He might not always make this apparent—there is a reason for this. I'm seeing he has an acute awareness that shapes his world as well as the world of his person, JC.

This is why he came into JC's life: to help JC build her awareness of security and safety.

He's protecting the energy for JC on levels beyond the physical. Oscar is his person's energetic caretaker and lighthouse keeper. He's part of JC's heart and soul in ways that have yet to be discovered. This is all in the bear's pace and the eye of the calculating eagle.

Right now he is telling me he is still getting his feet on the ground from his past. I am letting him know he has arrived and to trust how much he and JC know.

I'm seeing that there's a lot of gratitude coming from his soul to his person.

Intuitive Wisdom from Oscar to JC

Keep in mind, life is tenuous, strong, and situations in life will never falter as long as you move forward and do not waddle in the past. Stay in the present time for healing to occur.

I had to do this prior to coming to you. I had to remain present at all times, and I still remain present because it's so important. I learned a lot from that experience.

I want to teach you more about being in the moment and not going into the past or into the future wisdom too fast. I'm here to help guide you.

There is a lot of beauty in this world, and you see it. That's why we are together. We both see beauty and wisdom. We both see the intuitive potential of the world and of ourselves.

We are here to work together with our hearts and with our souls, to not only change one spot on this earth but to affect everything around us. I bring joy. I bring happiness. I bring healing. I bring awareness. I bring soul-level teaching to only those who listen.

I knew you were going to listen, and this is why I came. It's important that we are having our Wisdom Session today because our purpose needs to be clarified as to what we are doing together.

We can walk together every single day. Time doesn't matter as we are always working together. Keep this in mind when you are not physically with me.

When you meet someone for the first time, check in with me telepathically. My energy is here. Make sure we are aligned before you make any decisions. This way we can help each other.

I thank you for the rescue and for bringing me home. I love my home with you, and I love the work that we're doing.

I also like to have fun. The balance occurs when we don't have to think about the world at large. When we don't have to think about changing ourselves. When we have a lightness of being—an incredible amount of light and lightness.

To be able to feel the joy of the world and feel our own joy is what matters. We are a good match. I love this. I love that I have arrived to help you. I know you're helping me feel secure in my life.

I am giving the sense of security back to you too! Together let's do this! We can do this! Never forget wisdom. It's beautiful and it's healing.

We are onto something, my friend. Let's continue to move forward and not forget who we are in our wisdom. Let's bring who we are forward from the present to our NOW. We can do this—we are strong—we will never give up on our own work!

I want to be sure you understand that even though this is somewhat serious business, balance is awareness too. We spend joyful time and silly time together—this is balance.

I know I said this before, but it's important for us to be silly. I want you to learn from me to feel the earth and put your feet on the earth strongly through me. I am also still working on this, and I would appreciate your help.

Through that lesson let's teach each other to evenly ground ourselves—evenly feel the earth more to discover our souls together.

Because we are one, keep in mind that as a rescue I do not have regrets about my past. I hope I can teach you not to have regrets about your past. Let's look at our pasts and say thank you for the lessons they have given us.

From the past we can garner the lessons of joy, love, hope, and wisdom. Together we rescued each other and will work together to gain a foothold on our surroundings in our physical and earthly planes. We will develop and feel the joy while experiencing the seriousness of life. I love you, and thanks for giving me this gift to talk. I have been waiting for a long time.

Respectfully joyful,

Oscar

Love Note to Oscar from JC

Dear Oscar,

I am so grateful we had the opportunity to talk via Wendy. I love that you wanted to talk and that you are so wise!

Your Wisdom Message is very beautiful and timely. It has given me hope and joy for our life together.

It's such a relief to know you have not suffered a lasting hurt from your life in Romania and you live every day in the present with a huge capacity for fun.

I love you—my little "bear" dog—with all my heart!

Mindful togetherness,

JC

Critical Insight

An essential element that Oscar communicates, one relevant to so many of us, is:

Remain present for building awareness, strength, and hope. This will bring healing and joy into your world.

21—Enlightened Trust

Your enlightened being will become filled with
light when you learn to trust your gifts.

—Rascal, the cat

Rascal is a domestic, shorthair cat, male, age 14. When he was rescued from a storm sewer, he so young and tiny that his eyes were still closed. He was bottle-fed by humans. He is living.

Intuitive Conversation with Wendy

I love his energy! Rascal is a rascal, for he lives up to his name. When I was connected in with our Spirit Teams, he was actually singing to each of my Animal Spirit Team (see glossary for definition) members.

He is showing me a joyful soul. He's happy. He has a love of life, something not many felines will show me so immediately.

I'm seeing he has a passion for life and happiness. Yet, there's also a serious side to him. He demands, in a fair manner, respect, honor, and attention when he speaks.

Because he is clear, direct, and forthright, his person, CB, knows when he's feeling good and when he is not. He says this is how he can help CB too.

He assures me that his person know these sides of him well. Sometimes CB's emotions are a reflection of what Rascal is feeling. But there are times Rascal reflects CB's emotions as well. This mirroring is important for CB to pay attention to.

Intuitive Wisdom Message from Rascal to CB

Here is what I have to say and offer you as your teacher, sage, and coach in life. I'm here to help. Thank you for taking me into your heart and soul and arms after I spent time in that strange place. I don't have much recollection, but I can remember my littermates who were there with me.

My gratitude is important for you to hear. Thank you for rescuing me, bringing me into your life, and allowing me to develop into who I am.

I know I have a joyful soul, but I'm also serious. This is something that I want to sharpen within you. I ask you to allow yourself to feel more joy in your soul when you're not feeling good about yourself.

You are an amazing soul—an amazing person. Your heart is large, and your wisdom is large. You will continue to help people—that's your life's work.

I am here to guide you. To help you feel secure and confident in your work. I have no doubt where you're going in your work. You are an intuitive person, but sometimes you don't trust your intuition. Find the joy in your intuitiveness. Let my presence wrap your wisdom into a cocoon of warmth.

You will soar through the world as you learn to trust in your joy and beauty. Your heart will soar through the energy; it will keep your soul within your body.

Your enlightened being will become more filled with light when you learn to trust your gifts. I don't doubt myself because of you. You gave me trust, and now I want to give you trust too.

Do not doubt. Keep in mind that you have yet to discover everything you have to discern, but it's there for you at your fingertips. Look to me when you want to discover those things. Ask me because I can give you the confidence. I can give you the joy, and I can give you seriousness needed to learn. Never give up on yourself! You are an amazing person, CB!

Thank you so much for everything you are doing to allow me to be myself and develop into a wonderful cat. I am aware of my growth towards balance.

Keep in mind, balance in life is what's most important. Take your time. Respect your joy and your heart. Take your time with this concept. It's not about rushing; it's not about the end goal; it's about the process for you.

I understand the process really well, and if you want to see that through my eyes, my heart, and my soul, join me as we work together. I will continue to teach you balance, strength, and patience. I want to teach you—just like you taught me.

Guidingly yours,

Rascal

Love Note to Rascal from CB

Dear Rascal,

Thank you for explaining to me that you don't doubt yourself because of the trust I placed in you.

Your words of wisdom helped me realize why and how I need to learn to trust my gifts and that whatever I need to discover is there for me at my fingertips—provided I can overcome my hesitancy to trust myself.

With loving trust always,

CB

Critical Insight

An especially resounding message from Rascal to his person, one that is meaningful to so many of us, is:

Never give up on yourself! Your gifts are important!

22—Easing Self-Judgment

Your potential is great. You know the move-
ments. You are learning the connections for
growth.

—Francis, the cat

Francis is alive and is 12 years old. He is a domestic, shorthair, orange tabby. He was adopted from a shelter.

Intuitive Conversation with Wendy

Before I even begin to connect in with Francis he is saying to me, "Hey you over here! Hey you over here!" He wants full attention from me. He also asks me if I notice how handsome he is.

"Oh my," I say, "Of course I see your handsomeness."

He replies, "Well then, of course I will talk with you today."

I ask him why he wants such demanding and full attention. Why is it important for him to have his handsomeness acknowledged?

He comes back with, "Such a typical human concern."

As I continue to connect with him I am literally laughing out loud. I just love his commanding and fruitful ways of trying to divert my connection with him. I ask him if he would mind just waiting for further conversation, so we can connect. He complies.

A few minutes pass.

As I connect in now with Francis I am brought to his strength, his directness, his demanding but attractive demeanor. He is a pure energy without all the extras. You know where he stands and that he is a clear vessel for communication.

I am enjoying this connection. Francis is opinionated, but his opinions are well received by the Spirit Teams. He tells me he is opinionated because he is still working on understanding humans. He tells me we are complicated, and it's difficult for him to understand where we are coming from. This uncertainty gives trial to his self-confidence.

I agree with him and add he is not alone with his feelings. Many animals I have conversed with have the same experience and challenge. I tell him that his person came into his life to help him understand people better.

His energy completely shifts. His face lights up, and he turns to look at me. He becomes interested and not aloof. He wants to know and learn more.

He also tells me he is tactile—especially his whiskers. His whiskers are important to him, and he asks me if I like them. I tell him they make him look handsome. Of course, he likes this validation.

Intuitive Wisdom Message from Francis to MB

Well, hello there. Wendy saw how handsome I am. Do you see that? You are not looking deep enough. Stop what you are doing right now. Stop listening to this conversation. I want you to take a breath and bring your soul from the outside in. When you accomplish this, then begin again.

If at anytime you find yourself outside your body, please stop and go inside again. Find your place of mindful absorption before you read more.

This is the way I ask you to take in my words of wisdom to you.

I want to ask you—do you know why it is so important for me to remind you of why I am handsome? Why am I demanding that of you and why it is coming up in this conversation so insistently?

I promise you it's not to be silly, vain, or to be diverting the joy of this message. The purpose of me bringing this up within this conversation is to remind you to pay attention to your own self-judgment and be mindful of our surrounding beauty.

You see, we both share in a Soul Promise to steadfastly remain true to our own intensity of self-love. This is how I hope to teach you in this lifetime. I am aware of your self-judgment, and my job is to mirror these emotions back to you as a reminder for you to pay attention to your life's work.

When you listen to me with complete attention, you give me the respect of why I am here. You give me the opportunity to grow. When our souls come together, this concept will get us both further into our truth and purpose.

I keep bringing my looks up because this symbolism can be a perfect reminder for you when you judge yourself or feel unsure if you look beautiful. It is a reminder to bring your thoughts inside. When you have these sensations, stop yourself and go right past those doubts. Go to the place of inner truth and harmony. Hold me and look into my soul. Watch my whiskers as you meditate into mindfulness.

I'm being clear about this for you. Your potential is great. You know the movements; you are learning the connections for growth. I am your Soul Kitty to get you to a deeper place of self-understanding with attention to inner soul love.

The attention doesn't come from the outside world. Your fulfillment doesn't come at the expense of yourself or the opinions of others. Your attention comes from within. Pay attention to that which is within you and to the beauty within your soul. Pay strict attention.

We are great souls learning the direction of our path. I am a fair teacher that will guide you towards inner reflection and self-purpose. I am here to secure your inner being with strength, mental health, will, and details.

Handsomely yours,

Francis

Love Note to Francis from MB

Dear Francis,

You are my handsome comedian! I love how you lighten me up every moment of every day. I appreciate your beautiful, luminous light and ridiculously adorable antics.

Thank you for your brilliant, yet doable instructions on how to ground and connect with your wisdom (while I focus on your whiskers), which in turn helps me to reconnect to my own inner peace and harmony.

You have the smartest whiskers ever!

Love,

MB

Critical Insight

Let's all give attention to this insight from Francis:

Fulfillment comes when your attention grows from within. This awareness will bring harmony.

23—Two Lionesses

Remember your power and strength as you move through your world as any self-respecting lioness would.

—Miss Electra, the cat

Miss Electra was adopted from a shelter at age 13. She was almost 15 when she died. Miss Electra was a tabby. She was in the spirit world when we connected.

Intuitive Conversation with Wendy

Miss Electra communicates to me that the intensity in her eyes is not because she is trying to thwart our connection. Instead it's a deliberate, conscious choice for her to connect with me in this manner.

As we connect with each other Miss Electra sees immediately that I understand where she's coming from and that I can see that she honestly doesn't have much use for the folly of people. As she puts it, "People waste so much precious time with their constant fluctuations. It is entertaining, but most of the time I find it exhausting."

She goes on to relate, "I am here to tell you, I am direct. Oftentimes snarky with others and myself when I was here in the physical. But that isn't all of me. I have a great side too! But that great side doesn't waste time either."

Miss Electra will show her other side when we talk with her person. But still, her wisdom is her greatest attribute. It is solid, fair, forthright, honest, and direct.

She wants to help her person, CD, save time and streamline her abilities. Miss Electra points out that while all the other cats try to help CD, if CD would listen fully and without delay to her, then CD's journey could move in a streamlined and easy fashion.

"I mean, look at me," Miss Electra points out, "You can see how I streamlined my journey in the afterlife after I died. I didn't hang around for long in the transition period."

Miss Electra is showing me a clear and direct personality with consideration for her person's journey as well.

Intuitive Wisdom Message from Miss Electra to CD

When I died, I moved quickly and efficiently to the work that I am doing now in the afterlife. It was meant to happen that way. Please don't worry, as this was my path.

I want to thank you for bringing me home. I wasn't doing much at the shelter. I was lonely and frustrated that there was no one to talk to. The other felines were not interested, nor were the people, in conversing.

I knew you were coming for me. While I waited for you, I learned a lot about how to stay true to my own inner choices and direction. I also learned about being patient, which helped me with you during our short time together.

When I died, it didn't mean I left you unnoticed or abandoned you. This process was purely my way and my destiny to move quickly through the universe. Since my teachers are all about streamlining and moving through energy spaces quickly and without attachment—it was my chance to finally see that I could do so myself. Thank you for taking me in so I could fully learn what this was about.

My teachings for you are about mindful streamlining without attachment to those things, thoughts, and events that may slow down your confidence. Be the true lioness in your inner world.

My gift of intuitive spiritual wisdom is to always remind you to be mindful of this aspect of your human-ness. This is what my spirit energy did and is still doing for you.

I came into your life simply to help you move with grace and deliberation to get to your final destination, whether that is a decision, act, or choice that needs to be made. My life with you was filled with the beauty of this.

Honestly, I am not here today to give you a step-by-step approach. You clearly get that from the other cats in our family. It is nice to see you working on their teachings.

Instead, I am here to give you the kindness and the direction as a fair lioness so that you may have choices with your mindfulness that move you to a place of being efficient.

All the felines in your world and in your past are here to help. But I want you to know now—in no way do they compare with me. And I suspect this applies to the felines of your future as well. I am truly the lioness in your pride. I am your confidence and strength in terms of the essentials that you need.

I can see you not trusting this in yourself and that your confidence waivers sometimes. It is useful for you to revisit my message to you and remember that you were able to figure this out when I was with you in the physical.

Also, hear the roar of your voice as you express yourself. Don't hold back.

I do want to apologize if I drove you crazy sometimes. It was my way of helping you to understand what you needed to pay attention to. You needed that push. And I can see that you still do at times. There is much for you to learn and live, but all of us are here for you.

Remember your power and strength as you move through your world as any self-respecting lioness would. We move together with the graceful care needed that will lead us to our decisions, acts, and choices. This will streamline us to the beautiful mindfulness that universal energy has to offer.

With strength,

Your lioness,

Miss Electra

Love Note to Miss Electra from CD

Dear Miss Electra,

Your synergistic message about receptivity to the beautiful mindfulness that universal energy has to offer is my reminder to embrace my power and strength. These reminders will influence my decisions, acts, and choices.

When you mentioned a "self-respecting lioness," I knew that your symbolism contained a path to lead me to a deeper appreciation of my strength.

Synergistically yours,

CD

Critical Insight

Let's take a moment to revisit this powerful component of Miss Electra's message:

When you move with grace and deliberation, you will reach a decision with confidence and appreciation.

24—The Whispers of Our Souls

*I love the peace of our hearts and the whispers of
our souls. I know you can hear them too.*
                                    —Thomas, the cat

Thomas is a 12-year-old domestic, shorthair, black-and-white
tabby. He was adopted from a shelter. He is living.

Intuitive Conversation with Wendy

Thomas begins by sharing, "Wendy, I have had a good life. As
you can see from my energy I am content, and my energy
force is strong. I have seen a lot and heard a lot in my many
eventful years."

Thomas continues, "Since I have been fortunate to be given a
wonderful home where I live my daily life, I choose to do so
with utmost care and fastidiousness. I don't like messiness,
whether in my environment or within my spiritual soul. I know
neatness is not always possible, but it's what I believe to be
important to discuss today."

He continues to explain what he means by communicating:
"When you look at my energy, you can see how my colors
move around and through me. You can see how they make
deliberate, conscious shapes, and intentions. I am able to
direct these colors and shapes in order to have my

environment make sense. This vision allows me to see the energetic world as neat and orderly. Since I love life in the physical world, you would think I would choose to see differently. That is not the case."

Thomas indicates that what he wants to teach his person is that life, according to his perspective, is clear, direct, and intentional. There is honesty to the colors and shapes that are projected by any living being.

Intuitive Wisdom Message from Thomas to MB

There are so many things to explore in my physical life with you. I honestly have no intention of wanting this to change. I love our connection. I love the way we blend our daily lives to make sense of things. I love the safety and warmth you provide for me.

You have provided for me in a way that has allowed me to learn about the politeness of life. The softness and trust for my Spirit Team. With this growth my hopes are that I can further help you discover and implement your Spirit Team. Their energy is great for you.

This all flows so nicely for me. I love the peace of our hearts and the whispers of our souls. I know you can hear them too. In the stillness of our joined universe we have come to an honored place with each other. The time continues to move forward as we grow in our wisdom.

With this harmony there is still time for you to be human. It's still necessary. I understand this. And I also understand the challenges of being human.

I was sent to you to help you be confident and calm with your human-ness. I would like to remind you there are ways to make the physical world easier to navigate. I can see this energy around you. You acknowledge some but have not acknowledged all. This is your task.

I do have ways in which I can help you move through your world a little more easily if you are so inclined to have a conversation with me. Since I am a polite gentleman, I don't want to force anything upon you. That is not my way of teaching. My way of teaching is for a complete, utterly profound, and ultimate transformation for you.

I, like you, believe it takes time for change. It takes the beauty of mindfulness to move through each step of detection and unearthing. For you to have brief sightings of your potential is something to be aware of and trust. These are signs from your Spirit Team.

I know this all might seem like a simple and easy thing to do and even say. But I am not about to give you directions that don't have meaning for you. The simplicity of this message is actually complex because as you find your truth your answers will be encountered with profoundness.

I would like to ask to take your time with your journey. Take one step at a time for full recovery from one aspect of your life to the next. You can do this if you understand the process of listening to your own inner guidance in order to take that next mindful step.

When you do this, you are being polite to your Spirit Team. Your Spirit Team has many ways in which it can help you. Your five-member team is there for you when you want them to help you with patience, humbleness, and extremely polite mindfulness on your journey—if you trust them.

There are ways for you to converse with your Spirit Team that show great respect. First and foremost, when you listen for their answers, trust what they are telling you; then you are embracing their relationship with you.

If you are impolite, your Spirit Team will shut down to you. When they do this, you may feel confused, frustrated, and even alone. Keep in mind, when you ask them too many times the same question and you show uncertainty or the lack of willingness to trust their answer, then there will be no answer to your question. And your search will continue until you are ready to hear them.

This is all okay, and please do not dismay as your Spirit Team will give you only the answers you are ready for.

I am appreciative of your compassion and dedication to keeping me well feed and warm. I have great honor and respect for you.

With great respect and politeness,

Thomas

Love Note to Thomas from MB

Dear Thomas,

Thank you for the tender, gentle, and WISE Wisdom Session for me. I have been searching for a Spirit Guide (see glossary for definition) to help me understand the energetic, non-physical world better. Little did I know this teacher was furry, sitting on my lap, and staring at me with his gorgeous, soulful eyes!

Your teachings are a direct answer to my prayers, and I am so eager to be your willing student, with Wendy's help, of course.

You Wisdom Message confirmed what I always felt about you—you are a brilliant soul gifted to me from the heavens.

Delightfully your student,

MB

Critical Insight

When Thomas communicates the following to MB, it's an insight we all benefit from:

As time continues you will grow by moving forward with knowing your wisdom.

25—On Friendship

Our uniqueness and our story have numerous facets for growth and development.

—Peetie, the cat

Peeti was found in SB's garage. She was 3 years old when she died. She was white with black fur patches. I connected to her in the afterlife.

Intuitive Conversation with Wendy

As soon as I make connection with Peetie (it happens quickly), she starts to talk, which is one of her favorite things to do. She is a combination of a dear heart, wild child, and serious philosopher. Her energy is beautiful.

Peeti explains she lives a mindful life now—just as she did in her physical life.

Peeti has been waiting to talk with her person, SB, again because she misses SB. She misses hearing SB's voice as well as the companionship. What she misses most is the times when SB would explain to her project details that SB was involved in. She was intrigued by SB's words, thoughts, and decisions. She tells me that SB is a good teacher with a kind heart.

She says humans aren't really that interesting to her. They are slow to pick up on concepts and thoughts (even though humans are animals too, and it's important to remember this). Animals like her, and especially cats, are aware of many things that humans aren't. That is okay though, and there is a purpose for why she came into her person's life.

Peeti was checking out other households to spend her life with, but there was an energy calling her to come to SB. She knew there was work for both her and her person to do together.

She tells me, "There were lessons from SB that I was going to learn, and, of course, there were lessons I was going to teach him. I want you to please tell SB I am still close, and I check on him often. I'll make it easy for him. I can still be found in the basement and only there."

Intuitive Wisdom Message from Peeti to SB

SB, thank you for sharing your warmth and your heart with me. I know our spirits are connected on a soul level. Others may not completely understand, and that is okay.

Our friendship is between us. Your grief is between you and me as well. Remember, our bond is unique and complex. For us not to be together in the physical is difficult for the both of us.

Grief is like this for souls like us. Since our companionship is based on "rescuing" each other and building trust within our own beings, not having the physical connection requires us to rely on the strength of our energetic connection and build from there.

I knew when I found your garage, I had arrived at the home of my Soul Companion, a human who would gather the energy around me and help me be comfortable in body, mind, and spirit. You rescued me from that chaos.

I knew our Soul Promise was going to be fulfilled in this lifetime together. We asked the universe to bring us together because we understand each other. The universe noticed our equal intellect, and it was time for us both to come together and begin the work.

Yes, there were other places I could have chosen. But I was guided to you and I listened.

Our uniqueness and our story have many facets of growth and development. We learned to inquire and then trust. We learned to have a companionship that pulsed and flowed as if nothing else mattered.

You agree with me; I can see that clearly.

I came to you because I know we share similar goals for the purpose of healing our souls.

There was a glint in your eyes that I remember when we solved the greatest mystery. Our intelligent minds always wanted to know the answer. In our conversations we wanted solutions. In our trust we aimed to reach our hearts with compassion.

Our individualism is/was meant to be bonded in energy for as long as you wish. Our lessons of inquiry, trust, and companionship are why I am here for you still. We completed what we needed to complete in the physical, yet there is more for us to share.

I am still with you to remind you that within your inquires to life situations, issues, problems, and solutions, your true brilliance comes to fruition when you gather our mindfulness as a whole force. This gathering of mindfulness will tame the grief and loss, and continue to build your innate trust for yourself. You will continue to have companionship with your own mindfulness.

Within our continued conversation,

Peeti

Love Note to Peeti from SB

Dear Peeti,

Even though you were with me for three short years, I had a chance to hear you and understand how much meaning you had. You were a soulful force as we spent time in our basement dwelling. I am glad we found each other.

Thank you for showing up in my dreams and thoughts to let me know all is all right.

Your pal,

SB

Critical Insight

It's noticeably profound and relevant to all of us when Peeti points out:

Gathering mindfulness will tame your grief and loss. Having compassion for your mindfulness journey will continue to build your innate trust for yourself.

26—Beauty as Healing

See the beauty in everything before you consider another thought, observation, or choice. The beauty will unfold as our hearts unfold.

—Ruby, the dog

Ruby was a mini-dachshund female. She was adopted at the age of 2. At the time of this Animal Wisdom session Ruby was 14 years old, living, and in hospice. She is now deceased.

Intuitive Conversation with Wendy

The power of Ruby's song and soul is strong. She has wisdom and much to say. She talks about the beauty in the world and in her heart. The beauty in her person's heart is strong as well, and she wants to remind her person, CM, of many things.

Ruby is strong with this message, saying she has tremendous power within her big soul. Her little body holds a lot of power and energy—that's why she is still alive today.

The other thing I'm seeing: she is uncomfortable in her body. She often leaves her body to relieve the discomfort. Ruby believes in her body, and she's holding on.

Intuitive Wisdom Message from Ruby to CM

Recognize beauty everywhere you go NOW. Be aware of everything around you. Keep this foremost in your mind. Because after I am gone, I am going to continue to ask and demand of you to always recognize the beauty in life and all things.

When you're walking down the street, if you see a little butterfly, a blade of grass, or even a speck of earth dirt, always look for the beauty first. Look to the beauty first.

My personal medicine is beauty, love, kindness, and comfort. I'm about being safe and not having a higher expectation for the world. My patience has no expectation for you or myself.

I give you the ability to be yourself and to go through this life without having expectations that are unattainable. Even though I was well loved by my former people, they had a large expectation of me. Keep that in mind as you spend time and continue to work with me. My lesson is still here for you, even in hospice. Your patience with me is appreciated.

I am ready to go as I have completed my work here.

I am concerned about you. Please remember the love in the world. Even when I die, the love that I can give you will never go away. This is important for you to know.

We came into each other's lives at an important time. You gave me the universal promise to be able to live a life of comfort, fairness, respect, and love for life. You allowed me to be myself.

Life is a challenging journey, but I encourage you to now take those gifts that you gave me, along with my soul, into your soul in a new and different way. See the beauty in everything before you consider another thought, observation, or choice. The beauty will unfold as our hearts unfold—as we forever relive our passions together. Our intuitive bond is strong.

In beauty always,

Ruby

Love Note to Ruby from CM

Dear Ruby,

Thank you for giving me a prophetic message about savoring the memories of all the animals that have graced my life. Because of your words, I am remembering the great times and tucking those into my heart, seeing each as beautiful—with hope to bring back a chromatic life perspective.

Your Wisdom Message was empathic and a true reflection of your soul. Thank you for your strength and understanding.

I will always love and miss you!

With beauty,

CM

Critical Insight

Ruby's words are truly resounding. Let's revisit this sentiment:

See the beauty in everything before you consider another thought, observation, or choice.

27—Healing through Voice

Hear the voices of the universe that will enlighten your self-expression, creativity, and assertiveness. This all will be utilized in healing.
—Miss Luna, the cat

Miss Luna is estimated to be between 3 and 5 years old. She is a domestic, shorthair female. She is a rescue, and she's living.

Intuitive Conversation with Wendy

As I connect in with Miss Luna she immediately begins climbing all over me. She loves to talk, she tells me. It reduces stress, she assures me. She tells me if she holds her voice in, she isn't able to receive and contemplate the energy around her. Chattering away, she continues to connect with energy.

She is talking about everything and fast. Everything she is saying is important and not needless chatter. All her words have been well considered and predetermined (although I'm seeing she seems to show stagnant energy towards the base of her occiput, part of her throat chakra).

Right now she wants to share so much with her person, CD. Presently, she is going so quickly, I honestly can't keep up with her words. I sit patiently and let her get her words out, as she needs to use her voice.

My Spirit Team tells me this is important for her. This conversation is helping her balance her energy. She is in harmony with her surroundings, but there is something that has been blocking her flow. For her to talk right now is a cleansing thing and a healing act for her.

Miss Luna is a sweet kitty. She is feminine and kind. She is steadfast in her opinions and in her ways. Deep down she holds a soft and sweet spot. And a warm spot of deep concern and value for all that comes into her life.

Her talking is slowing down now, and she is thanking me for the opportunity to get her words out. She loves sharing her words of wisdom, care, and concern. She tells me she was holding her words in a lot because she didn't want to disturb her person or the other cats in her family.

Family is important to her. In her young age she tells me her words may sound like chatter to many, but in reality they are critical. She appreciates being respected and listened to.

She gives me a little smile and a little wink. She feels more confident now and is relieved she doesn't have to try so hard.

She also tells me she likes to climb and find places to hide.

When she hides, it's not to get away from things but for her to contemplate her next move or reflect on a new piece of wisdom.

She also tells and shows me the place in her throat chakra again where the energy is stagnant. She asks if I can help.
I explain that I can, but that we should ask her person to help her first. She likes that idea a lot.

Wisdom Message from Miss Luna to CD

Did you know that you are a healer? I am here to guide you. You are able to help animals with your hands and guide their energy. I want you to help me by listening to this Wisdom Message with your Spirit Team.

First I ask that you continue to work on healing your own soul and areas of difficulty. Yes, I am going to be blunt with you and honest. This honesty comes from a place of warmth and compassion that you guided me to embrace.

I have energy like no other cat in our household, but oftentimes because I am young, I am not heard. This is similar to you and your experiences in life. Those experiences where you feel as if you have the wisdom to share and help but are not heard by those that could benefit.

[Note from Wendy to CD: since the strongest energy is coming from Miss Luna's throat/occipital region, she would like to talk to you about that in great detail. However, this Animal Wisdom session is not so much about her stagnant energy in the throat/occipital region; it is more about your energy and working step by step to heal yourself.]

I would like for you to pay attention and be mindful of this area. Not only in the occipital region but the entire throat chakra area. I would like you to expand your energy out to include at least ten feet in all directions of your physical body. You can do this in meditation and when you are in need of strength and introspection. It's important for you to visualize this area in this way first. Practice this without rushing. It will become a priority.

Once you understand and incorporate this into your mind's eye you will feel confident the universe is hearing you.

Please then visualize your organs and body structures in this area. Visualize and see deeply what your thyroid looks like. Look at your neck in general and how it appears to be. Remember your ears and your atlas.

Take your time with this. Do not rush through this process. The time it takes to open and clear the communication channels for your feelings and thoughts is ongoing. I ask you to look for stillness, respect, and communication with and for yourself.

This practice will stimulate your creativity in regard to speaking up, releasing, breathing your life force, and healing. You will contain the needed energy to move yourself forward. This energy is needed for your own healing and then for the healing of others, especially animals.

Be mindful when your self-expression shuts down or you are hesitant to speak your feelings because of judgment. Your frustrations will build if you don't. Look for guidance and support.

Remember, always be aware of your place in the physical world. Please pay attention to your voice and hear the voices of the universe, which will enlighten your self-expression, creativity, and assertiveness. This all will be utilized in healing.

Remarkably me,

Miss Luna

Love Note to Miss Luna from CD

Dear Miss Luna,

You are helping me continue to grow and learn from my self-expression, creativity, and assertiveness.

Your words of wisdom remind me that paying attention to my voice and listening to the guidance of the universe would enhance my ability as a healer.

I appreciate your dedication to give me the courage to pursue my dream of helping others heal from loss.

Healing together,

CD

Critical Insight

An essential element that Miss Luna imparts that is relevant to so many of us is:

When you pay attention to your own voice, your soul will be enlightened. You will then have a companion for your healing journey.

28—Slow Appreciation

Feel your feet dig into the earth, take a deep breath, and clear your lungs.

—Riley, the dog

Riley is a male Brittany and is 20 months old. He is a rescue. He is living.

Intuitive Conversation with Wendy

As Riley comes in with his energy it sweeps me up. He has the energy of a gazelle running. He is showing me his high spirit, boundless energy, fast running, and intent sniffing, all the while being totally absorbed in his doggy world. Not staying in one place for a long time. Even when resting he is moving around a lot.

He honestly doesn't want to slow down to talk with me because he is always on a mission, so he tells me. I ask if I can view his doggy world at the lightening speed he is going.

"Sure, if you can keep up. I don't want to wait," he responds.

I respect this and join his approach.

In his way he is showing me a lot about his life and the way he lives it. He tells me this fast motion is common in his everyday life. He tells me that moving fast is how he buffers himself. It's difficult for him to feel grounded.

He wants his person, SF, to join in with his energy more and learn from him. When SF does this, it will help both parties. When SF meets him this way, SF will be able to communicate with him with less chaos.

He's good with this. He really likes his person, and he thinks his person is fun. Energy is showing me he views SF as a playmate and as younger than him in energy.

It is difficult for Riley to come down to speak from his high-energy source. This is not a bad thing, but he needs SF to look at him differently, communicate with him differently, and meet him where he is at energetically. When this happens, he can release some of this protectiveness he has built around himself. He is moving this fast because this is the way he feels safe.

I am also picking up a food allergy to chicken. There are more, but this is what Riley shows me now. Food allergies and other allergies can alter energy in the physical, mental, and spiritual realms.

Intuitive Wisdom Message from Riley to SF

First, I would like to say thank you for setting up this conversation. I know I have to move fast right now because this energy is new for me. Plus I have a hard time slowing down, and I would like you to help me.

No one has ever respected me before. No one has every taken the time to hear what I have to say. Many have had high expectations of me on their terms. You know what I mean, right? You feel that way as well sometimes—that you are not being heard as you would like and others have set high expectations for you that are not fair or reasonable.

We are going to help each other, as this is our Soul Promise.

Something we share and part of the reason for this fast energy is we both move too fast in our thoughts and in our daily lives. It's difficult for people to hear what we have to say—or even want to hear what we have to say. But if you and I slow down together and help each other, our messages and conversations will be heard. I would really like that.

I know you are wise and know how to do this better than I do, so I need your help. Do you know why? Like Wendy told you, one of the reasons I move fast is because I feel the need to take everything in and if I move fast, I will stay out of the energetic path of judgment from others. Right?

But in reality, when I slow down, like I have now to talk with you—I feel nervous and unsure of myself.

Now, I want you to do the same with me. Instead of doing a gazillion things at once and letting your mind take over your voice, I would like for you to be aware of yourself when you converge with me. Feel your feet dig into the earth, take a deep breath, and clear those lungs. Ask me to do the same in energy, not words. On the inside and eventually on the outside—I will settle. Please ask things of me; I will hear you as long as you are fully with me.

If your energy is running around fast and furious, then I will too! Even if I am not running fast and furious in the physical—inside I am. Then it will be impossible for our energies to blend, communicate, and deliver the appropriate change.

Thank you so much for this conversation. It is so nice now to be respected and heard.

Respectfully with you,

Riley

Love Note to Riley from SF

Dear Riley,

It was amazing to hear from you as to what makes you tick. This is so insightful for me. When we first brought you into our home, it was incredibly stressful and crazy. Your high energy and spirit were exhausting.

Our life together has been an evolution for sure, and now life with you is becoming a fun and treasured quality. We have settled into each other's lives.

For a young pup, you are observant, and your advice for me to focus on one or two things, rather than a "gazillion," will truly benefit me.

You are a love. Thank you for responding positively when I take time to be with you and let my mundane tasks wait.

With much appreciation,

SF

Critical Insight

It's a breathtaking insight and one that most of us should be reminded of when Riley remarks:

Instead of doing a gazillion things at once, be aware of yourself as you feel your feet dig into the earth. This will deliver your appropriate change.

29—Intuitive Gifts

I am going to ask you to try and not go beyond what your energy is ready for right now.
—Coco, the dog

Coco is a 6-year-old female beagle. She is not a rescue. She is living.

This is the second Intuitive Wisdom session for Coco and JS. The first conversation is in chapter 8.

Intuitive Conversation with Wendy

As I connect again with Coco she is jolly and enjoys the recognition from me. She enjoys the reconnection. She is telling me she learned a lot from our last conversation and is looking forward to fine-tuning it some.

Her first conversation was important and critical for her. I tell her we are excited to hear what else she has to tell us. Our reconnection for the purpose of conversation and wisdom delights her. She is attentive, grinning, and ready to talk!

There was a moment of surprise when I first connected with her. She was surprised to be asked again to talk. She tells me there was a lot to work on for JS, her person, in the first message, and it's still important for JS continue with those suggestions. But since she's a teacher that's lovable and endearing, she is feeling proud to be called upon again. This makes her feel important.

I ask her if there's anything in particular that is different from the first session that she'd like to tell me. She shares, "Wait and you will find out."

The energy presented by her is peaceful, neutral, and similar to that of the first session. The difference is that Coco's vision and energy is laser-focused from an innate spiritual place.

She reminds me she is happy and smart. Since she likes balance, having fun is important too. Fun and lightness is imperative for both Coco and JS together.

Intuitive Wisdom Message from Coco to JS

There are many things to consider when you ask about our mission together—with humans and wild animals.

Before this concept is translated to you I must share the importance of managing your energy. You cannot move forward without knowing and practicing this. It wouldn't be healthy for you.

Before moving forward with anything else it will be important for you to learn ways of self-preservation that are unique to you and your Spirit Team. They are there wishing to talk with you in daily life as well as with your healing work.

You have five Spirit Team members and five Animal Spirit Team members that will help you move forth in this world as a healing conduit for many people and animals. Knowing these guides will help you to discover your exact work and how to proceed with your work.

Right now I can see you working on mostly animals as this is where your passion lies. You will work with people as well, but I cannot share that with you right now. That information is not available for you yet.

Keeping your hands and the energy behind your hands full of pure, essential light with a background of wisdom will be the goal for you. This will be the challenge for you if you move forward with this choice.

As far as wild animals are concerned, it's too early to tell how you will pursue this work. There are many things that need to happen first. The one thing I can tell you is that I like to use my nose, and I wouldn't mind finding lost wild animals.

But this session is about the healing work you will be doing with your hands. This is not Reiki; this is discovering your own unique energy system by practicing on me and connecting in with your team. Trainings are good to do, but honestly you have more healing abilities than what is known.

I'm going to ask you to try and not go beyond what your energy is ready for right now. In the last conversation I told you it was important for you to listen to the world around you. It's important for you to listen to your intuition to trust you have a gift. But it's also important for you to manage your input and output.

The lesson is not to push your soul to do something before you have done the work to get there. You need a team to help you discover EXACTLY what your journey is.

Mom, I appreciate you and your desire to hear what I know about you. I want to help you, and I am glad you are listening to my voice.

Love,

Coco

Love Note to Coco from JS

Dear Coco,

I want to thank you for another beautiful conversation. Coco, I feel so loved by you.

As I move into a new phase of my life I know you are there with me. I feel your amazing being and wisdom by my side. Know I feel love from you.

With gratitude,

JS

Critical Insight

Coco sagely reminds us all of the importance of the following:

It is not necessary to push your soul to do something before you have done the work to get there. Your Spirit Team will help.

30—A Legend with a Soulful Heart

Happiness is about blending your beauty with your environment.

—Marley, the dog

Marley was a Samoyed. She died at the age of 12 from nasal-sarcoma. She was not a rescue and died too young, as she was completely healthy otherwise. Marley was my beloved animal. She was in the spirit realm when we made our connection.

Intuitive Connection with Wendy

When I connect with Marley, she is present for me. Her calmness, kindness, and gentle ways are opening our dialogue. There has never been a time when she didn't answer my request for a soul-level conversation.

Marley asked to be in this book because she wanted to continue to supply her wisdom of utter happiness. She is glad she is being included, as her Soul Promise is to help as many people as she can.

Since I communicate with her on a daily basis, our connection comes easily. Her beautiful "Sammy" smile warms our energy connection as we sit and ponder her Animal Wisdom Message to me.

Today Marley is coming forward as a compassionate teacher and a reminder of awareness.

Marley is reminding me how she shared her insightful doggie wisdom of universal kindness, calmness, and love to all who listen to her.

With great patience, intuition, gentle ways, and her huge, unselfish heart she taught all that she touched how to be a better human! The Divine Ms. M (Marley's nickname) was a true healer and a blessing.

She's ready to share her wisdom.

Intuitive Wisdom Message from Marley to Wendy

Happiness is about blending your beauty with your environment. Take in all you have learned from our time together and soar into the universe with your exquisiteness. This will keep you happy and healthy.

Please remember how real I was in my physical life. With being real I taught you to trust who you are and the decisions you make. Couple this with your intuition, and you are able to claim this as your reality and your gift from me.

When you are real with yourself and those around you, life will flow more easily. It may not seem true during a challenging time, but you know from experience this is true.

The awareness of truth is why I was able to help you learn how to buffer the obstacles that held you back. When you learned to recognize your obstacles, you began once again to move forward with your dance with life. I feel fortunate for being part of your loveliness and truth-bearing discoveries.

I know when I came into your life, you were unsure of who you were. You took brave chances that altered your truth. I stood by you and supported you to your moment of mindfulness where you discovered those choices that were challenging your truth.

Your fear to be happy was a huge block and contained you from swimming forward with your purpose in life. Life is not about being contained in a secure vessel. It's about revealing yourself to the beauty and being vulnerable with your fear.

I taught you to be brave with everything you do in life. You have accomplished much because you listened to me. Thank you for listening to me, as this was my Soul Promise for you. Because I accomplished my task, my work now is still in the afterlife. I work with those who wish for happiness.

I love that we have contact every day and you include me when consulting with clients. I see Kado [Marley's brother] also continues to work with you as well.

Remember that your inner critics are no longer powerful and convincing. In the past they had the ability to laser focus on your self-doubt. They tried to take over your mind with their chaos. But your strength didn't let them win.

Thank you for allowing me to fulfill my Soul Promise to you. Thank you for still conversing with me and helping me with your Soul Promise to me because we each learned to help those with fear so large it stopped them from being humane to themselves.

Your forever companion,

Marley

Love Note to Marley from Wendy

Dear Marley,

I hear your voice within my heart as I move through my days with self-kindness and appreciation. You gave me so much in life, and without you it would have taken me much longer to find my happiness. Thank you for being my continuing teacher.

Thank you for showing me how to feel brave with myself and how to take the plunge towards happiness. This lesson alone is invaluable.

I am fulfilling my life's purpose because of your generous teachings.

From fear to happiness,

Wendy

To my readers: if you would like to receive a Free Audio Chapter called "Don't Mess With My Happiness!" from my bestselling book, *Choosing Happiness*, please visit https://wendyvandepoll.com. This chapter tells the story of how Marley saved my life.

Critical Insight

Something Marley told me that I think resonates with so many people is:

Your inner critics are no longer powerful and convincing. They tried to take over your mind with their chaos. But your strength didn't let them win.

31—Lasting Wisdom

You and your beloved companion share or may have shared an astonishing life together. You might be constant companions roaming the world with great adventures, or perhaps you enjoy quiet times on the couch snuggling on a snowy day. Your bond may have provided solace, safety, and companionship.

No matter what your adventures are or were, how you spent your special moments, or how you offered emotional support for each other, you both created a unique conversation that shaped your eternal bond.

Your daily conversations with your beloved companion may go unnoticed, as they are at times subtle. Your animal companion can, at times, be profound and other times silly, but the ability for them to help you see things for what they truly mean can change the outlook you have on your life.

Without judgment, criticism, or intolerance, your animal listens to the secrets that you consciously or subconsciously share. There is an unspoken respect and confidentiality between the both of you.

Your animal is a master of unconditional love, both for themselves, the world they live in, and you. I learned this mostly from my dog Marley (chapter 30), but I experience this with every single animal I have had the honor to non-verbally speak with.

The biggest difference between our beloved companions and ourselves is how they approach daily living and their responses to events. As an animal communicator having thousands of conversations with both wild and domestic animals, I can tell you that living life in the present with a freeing soul is how animals experience happiness. And they want this for you too!

I have heard this from countless critters, ranging from wild wolves coming out of hiding to show me the safe way home, to a darling goldfish who desired her human to embrace his life and trust his intuition.

No matter the species or my relationship to the animals I have spoken to, they share a commonality in regard to their wisdom—our animals want to strengthen the human-animal bond by helping us become better at being human and humane.

When we listen to their wisdom and realize all animals in our lives have a pulse on life and us, we actually help them become healthier, better behaved, and better adjusted to being able to live with our foibles. And this is not by changing them, but changing ourselves! Consider, if you will, no animal has ever asked me to change them or their relationship to life! It was their person who was challenged with choices to change.

In my work I have animals wanting to help us by "acting out," "showing up anxious," and even showing signs of "illness" when conversing with me non-verbally. But for the most part, these scenes are not about them; these scenes are about the emotional states of their people.

In reality your animal is showing you and giving you answers to some of your most difficult decisions. Your animal is your teacher, wisdom-bearer, mentor, and guide who will insist that you take the next step on your journey to discovering your unique life path. They will challenge and push, so you will readily get answers to your questions that result in solutions.

The animal kingdom is present, and all animals have their ways that they share their voices with us. First and foremost they are fair and honest. But they are also strong and direct.

It isn't always easy to hear what they are telling us. Yet, we must keep in mind they come from a place of compassion and offer extreme patience when guiding us to a place of mindful balance. Everyone can hear the messages from their animals.

For centuries animals have been companions and teachers for us. They have offered us ways to evolve, yet it hasn't been easy for them to "get through" to our minds. Yet they persevere—even those that suffer through abuse, judgment, and lack of respect—to continue their work to help us.

This is dedication, and it's why for us animal lovers it becomes extremely difficult to deal with grief due to pet loss. Animals love all of life unconditionally.

I hope you enjoyed this book and were able to bring a loving heart and open mind as you read and experienced the profound Animal Wisdom Messages contained within.

Each animal suggested and agreed to sharing their knowledge publically with hopes that their words will help you find support, healing, and inspiration to mindfully listen to the words of the furred, feathered, and/or finned creature in your life.

Warmly,

Wendy Van de Poll, MS, CEOL

January 10, 2018

Glossary

Animal Communication—telepathic (see definition below) communication that involves the direct transmission of feelings, intentions, thoughts, mental images, emotions, impressions, sensations, and intuition (see definition below.)

Animal Communicator/Interspecies Communicator/Conversationalist—a person who has the ability to communicate with animals via their intuitive/psychic/medium skills. The animal doesn't need to be present. The information that they receive will be very detailed depending on the animal communicator. A skilled animal communicator goes beyond physical information and deals with Soul Contracts and Promises (see definition below). They can speak with those who have passed, as well as the living.

Animal Medium—another term for "animal communicator"; a person who has the ability to speak to animals that have died. Some animal communicators may speak to animals in spirit but not all. Many animal communicators offer both or specialize.

Animal Spirit Team—a group of five energetic animals (mostly wild animals) that come to each person at the moment of conception and stay with that individual until death. They work with each member of a person's Spirt Team. They help their individual to trust their intuition and decisions and to increase their relationship with the world at large. Wendy works closely with her clients to discover their Animal Spirit Team.

Animal Totem or Spirit Animal—an animal guide who appears to offer love, healing, and support. They appear in dreams, visions, and real-time meetings. They are not part of the five Animal Spirit Team members.

Animal Wisdom Message—telepathic interspecies communication between a human and their pet/companion/beloved animal friend. The intention of these messages from our animals is based on the Soul Promises (see definition below) we have with the animals in our lives. They reveal life path messages based on love, compassion, patience, mindfulness, and truth.

Chakras—seven energy centers in the body, human and animal, through which energy flows. They include the root, sacral, solar plexus, heart, throat, third eye, and crown. A chakra can be thought of as a vortex or whirlpool.

Intuition—something most people experience all the time that supply people with ideas, creative inspiration, feelings of apprehension, and more. Intuition strengthens and becomes clearer and stronger the more it is trusted and followed.

Soul Animal or Soul Pet—a furred, finned, or feathered companion that makes a Soul Promise (see below) to guide, enlighthen, inspire, etc., their human to become more humane to the world at large.

Soul Person—a human companion to a furred, finned, or feathered animal that makes a Soul Promise (see below) to support their animal companion with their joint agreement set forth prior to birth.

Soul Promise—agreements made prior to birth when all creatures, human and animal, exist in spirit form. During this time a person's higher self or soul selects lessons for the person to learn during their next lifetime that will assure the person will achieve the most soul growth as possible. Each person creates a life that will include many things—challenges, sadness, joy, loss, and achievements—that are special for that individual. The goal is to develop towards moving closer to unconditional love. There are many different types of Soul Promises.

Spirit Guides—energetic entities that come and go. They support the work of a person's Spirit Team (see definition below). Their job is to support a person with intuitive development, healing, and spiritual growth.

Spirit Team—a group of five energetic entities that come to each person at the moment of conception and stay with each person until death. They are considered a person's spiritual BFFs. They help each person with trusting their intuition, decisions, and increasing their relationship with the world at large. Wendy works closely with her clients to discover their Spirit Team (see resources).

Telepathy—the direct communication of thoughts and feelings between people or people and animals without the need to use speech, writing, or any other "normal" signals.

Universal Wisdom—acquired when working with your Spirit Team and Animal Spirit Team with intuition, intention, and change. It is when a person is fully committed to living life mindfully and with intention for the greater good.

Resources

Ways That Wendy Can Support You with Animal Communication

A Free Gift Awaits You!
https://wendyvandepoll.com

Animal Wisdom Message
https://wendyvandepoll.com/animal-wisdom-message

Animal Communication
https://wendyvandepoll.com/animal-communication

Animal Mediumship
https://centerforpetlossgrief.com/animal-medium

Discover Your Spirit Team
https://wendyvandepoll.com/services/discover-spirit-team/

Ways That Wendy Can Support You with Pet Loss Grief

Center for Pet Loss Grief: Through Life, Death, and Beyond
Wendy Van de Poll, MS, CEOL

A Free Gift from My Heart to Yours Awaits You!
https://centerforpetlossgrief.com

Free Pet Loss Grief Resources Packet
https://centerforpetlossgrief.com/resource-packet/

Support for Pet Professionals
https://centerforpetlossgrief.com/pet-professional-grief-support

Online Courses for the Pet Professional and Pet Lover
https://spiritpaw.academy

Pet Grief Support
https://centerforpetlossgrief.com/pet-grief-support

Pet Funerals
https://centerforpetlossgrief.com/pet-funeral

Animal Mediumship
https://centerforpetlossgrief.com/animal-medium

Animal Communication
https://wendyvandepoll.com/animal-communication

Facebook: Center for Pet Loss Grief
https://facebook.com/centerforpetlossgrief

Pet Memorial Support Group
https://facebook.com/groups/
petmemorials.centerforpetlossgrief

Marley's Life Celebration Video
https://youtu.be/1bXUoPTivxk

Veterinarians

Veterinary Medical Association
http://ahvma.org

Home Euthanasia and Pet Hospice Veterinarians
http://iaahpc.org

Online Product Support

BL Digital Media
https://bldigitalmedia.com/bl-life-celebration-videos/

Herbal Support: Pet Wellness Blends Affiliate
http://herbs-for-life-3.myshopify.com/#_l_1e

Magnetic Therapy Supplies: aVivoPur Affiliate
www.avivopur.com/#_a_CenterForPetLossGrief

Heart in Diamonds: Affiliate
http://www.heart-in-diamonds.com/?aff=CenterForPetLoss

Support Groups

Association for Pet Loss and Bereavement
http://aplb.org

International Association for Animal Hospice & Palliative Care
http://iaahpc.org

Association for Human-Animal Bond Veterinarians
http://aahabv.org

Acknowledgments

First, I would love to express my deepest appreciation to all my fellow colleagues—the animal communicators and pet care professionals who dedicate their lives to doing the best they can every day to increase the richness of the human-animal bond.

Thank you to the delightful animals, both two-legged and four, for sharing your wisdom, stories, growth, and love. This book has been an incredible journey for me, and I met so many powerful and insightful creatures. My life changed through your wisdom.

Thank you, Nancy Pile, my editor, who always brings my books to perfection with her eagle eye, full heart, and dancing paws. Thank you to Doug Heatherly, PhD, of Lighthouse24, for his exquisite formatting and to GermanCreative for her phenomenal book cover artistry.

To Addie, Marley, Kado, Maya, and the rest of my fur, feather, and fin family who continue to hold my heart through their uncanny conversations that keep me on my path of translating Animal Wisdom for those who listen. They are amazing and wise teachers. They never let me forget who I am.

To my husband, Rick—a scientist and poet who converses with the animals too!

About the Author

Wendy Van de Poll is a pioneering leader in the field of pet loss grief support and animal communication. Wendy is dedicated to providing a safe place for her clients to express their grief over the loss of their pets and increasing the human-animal bond.

What makes Wendy successful with her clients is that she gets animals! As Wendy shared, "Over the years I've helped many people communicate and connect with their pets to increase their bond for a richer life. It's what I've done since I was just 5 years old!"

She is compassionate and supportive to all who know her.

Wendy's passion is to telepathically talk to animals and help people when they are grieving over the loss of a pet. Her larger-than-life love for animals has led her to devote her life to the mission of increasing the quality of life between animals and people, no matter what their stage in their cycle of life! She has been called the "animal whisperer."

Wendy is a certified end-of-life and pet grief support coach, certified pet funeral celebrant, animal medium and communicator, and licensed massage therapist for human, horse and hound. She is the founder of The Center for Pet Loss Grief and an international bestselling and award-winning author and speaker.

Her courses are AAVSB RACE-certified, and she travels the country providing continuing education for veterinarian professionals.

Wendy holds a Master of Science in Wolf Ecology and Behavior, and has run with wild wolves in Minnesota, coyotes in Massachusetts, and foxes in her backyard. She lives in the woods with her husband, two crazy birds, her rescue dog, Addie, and all kinds of wildlife.

Wendy currently has a Skype, phone, and in-person practice, providing end-of-life and pet grief support coaching, animal communication and mediumship, and personalized pet funerals.

You can reach her at www.wendyvandepoll.com or www.centerpetlossgrief.com.

Thank You for Reading

Animal Wisdom:
*Conversations of the Heart between
Animals and Their People*

As the author of this book, I appreciate you buying and reading it. I hope that you found it to be helpful, as did the many others who shared their stories within its pages.

I would be grateful if you would leave a helpful book review, either with your favorite book distributor or with Amazon.

Thank you,

Wendy Van de Poll, MS, CEOL
Bestselling Author, Certified End-of-Life and Pet Loss Grief Coach, Animal Communicator and Medium, andFounder of The Center for Pet Loss Grief

www.centerpetlossgrief.com

www.wendyvandepoll.com

For all of Wendy Van de Poll's books, visit:

https://www.amazon.com/Wendy-Van-de-Poll/
e/B01BMUWX7O

Bestselling and Award-Winning Books
By Wendy Van de Poll, MS, CEOL

Pet Bereavement Series

My Dog IS Dying: What Do I Do?
My Dog HAS Died: What Do I Do?

My Cat IS Dying: What Do I Do?
My Cat HAS Died: What Do I Do?

Healing a Child's Pet Loss Grief

The Pet Professional's Guide to Pet Loss

Free Book

Healing Your Heart from Pet Loss Grief

Children's Picture Books

The Adventures of Ms. Addie Pants Series
    The Rescue
    The Ice Storm
    New Friends
    Off to School

To receive notification when more books are published, please go to

https://wendyvandepoll.com
or
https://centerforpetlossgrief.com

and we'll include you on the mailing list after you download your free gift.